ADVANCE PRAISE FOR DAN NICHOLSON AND RIGGING THE GAME

"Over the last few decades, I have helped gold-medal athletes, world champions and Fortune 500 CEOs get clarity on their goals, create certainty around achievement of outcome and collapse the timeframe to get there as fast as possible. In *Rigging the Game*, Dan Nicholson has masterfully broken down how to get clarity around your personal definition of wealth, feel certain that you'll achieve it and collapse the time so it happens faster than you ever thought possible."

-Dr. Jeff Spencer, Olympian and coach to Olympic athletes and Tour de France Gold Medalists

"As a business professor, executive coach and philanthropist, I have read over 2,000 books. Most are touted as the next big thing that is going 'revolutionize the field' of fill-in-the-blank. Every so often, one comes along that truly changes the land-scape. *Rigging the Game* is the real deal. It contains theories that are on par with anything from the top business schools, yet it goes much further by providing actual steps you can take to ensure success in your business and your life. The fix is in, and *Rigging the Game* is a real winner!"

-Randy Massengale, former Senior Advisor to Bill Gates at Microsoft, serial entrepreneur, professor and philanthropist

"Dan Nicholson has created the single most powerful operating system to help business owners get what they want out of life. I use it and teach it to all my clients."

-Nic Peterson, co-founder of Mastery Mode and author of *Bumpers*

"I have sought Dan's consultation on multiple occasions. His work has helped open my mind and shift my perspective to create real and personal financial change. This is *so* worth the read!"

-Dr. Gabrielle Lyon, founder of Muscle-Centric Medicine®, private doctor specializing in functional medicine

"It is impossible to overstate the extent to which Dan Nicholson's concepts, perspective and intellect have impacted my life. His lessons go way beyond learning experiences. Every time I have learned from Dan, I've felt elevated with a whole new view of life, business and finance and proceed as a new person with greater clarity and certainty. He has helped me close the gap between where I am and where I want to be much faster than I ever thought possible. My goals and aspirations no longer feel like long-term goals because Dan has helped me collapse time and see things through a whole new lens."

-Jeff Moore, founder of Thursday Night Boardroom, a global mastermind and entrepreneurial group serving members from 28 countries

RIGGING

THE

GAME

HOW TO ACHIEVE FINANCIAL CERTAINTY,
NAVIGATE RISK AND MAKE MONEY
ON YOUR OWN TERMS

Dan
Nicholson

LEGACY
launch pad
PUBLISHING

ISBN: 978-1-956955-44-6 (ebook)

ISBN: 978-1-956955-43-9 (paperback)

ISBN: 978-1-956955-45-3 (hardcover)

To my loves, Kim, Noella and Cora. Every action I take is to get closer to you.

Access Additional Free Resources and
Content Using the QR Code Below

CONTENTS

PREFACE

Entrepreneurship found me at an early age, although I didn't have a name for it at the time.

I was one of those kids who hustled to make and sell products. I had a knack for sales and understanding how commerce worked.

I also had mostly perfect grades (except for a period in high school when I tried to get away with doing next to nothing), scores of awards and a reputation as a relentless learner that was solidified in college. It seemed to me the path toward greatness meant counterbalancing my internal chaos with rigidity. So naturally, I pursued academic success. For a time, it worked out, or so it seemed. I got an accounting degree, supplemented with another in information systems because I thought it'd be the best skill set to start a business. But I got sidetracked.

I racked up record-breaking scores on tests and aligned myself with legendary financial institutions. I even helped write a national accounting standard. I somehow convinced myself along the way that all these vanity metrics—the titles, trophies and external praise—were noble pursuits, all in the name of getting one reward or another. My self-worth was tied up in accomplishing and doing, but inside, I felt a little misaligned and confused about where I was really *going*. I seemed to exist between many of the categories the world tends to put people into:

→ *Creative, but mathematically inclined*
→ *Introverted, but fiercely competitive*
→ *A quiet thinker and planner enamored with the idea of greatness*

Accountants put a lot of stock in standards like these, and it certainly should have felt like a major achievement that I was all of these things. Nonetheless, all of these positive outcomes couldn't relieve the apprehension I was feeling. I still felt myself pulled strongly in the direction of entrepreneurship, away from what was turning into a promising future in accounting (at least, on paper).

To compound the paradigm I was in, there was another, more self-sabotaging thought weighing on my mind. Aside from the impressive resumé I was earning, I was also the first in my family to go to a university. Anyone who comes from a similar situation knows that there is a certain kind of pressure that comes with this distinction. While my parents never put this expectation on me, I knew how much they sacrificed to give me the opportunities I encountered and how fortunate I was to be staring down such a lucrative career path in the first place.

In spite of all the progress I seemed to be making, my career was stuck in a loop. I changed course regularly, laughing off every dead end and pivot as a lesson learned from failure when the reality was I simply couldn't make up my mind.

Like many twenty-somethings, I dropped directly into a bit of a quarter-life crisis. I pinballed back and forth between what

I *knew* I wanted to do and what I felt I *should* be doing. I wanted to be an entrepreneur, not an employee.

No matter how much time I spent failing, attempting to learn from those failures and finding success in one corner or another, a lot of questions went unanswered:

- *How could I hit a home run one day and then strike out the next?*
- *How could I seemingly "do all the research" and then have the resulting idea just fizzle out?*
- *How could I be on the precipice of achieving everything I wanted only to restart days later?*

Meanwhile, it seemed other entrepreneurs regularly adopted the same approach as Captain Hernán Cortés in 1519 during the Spanish Conquest of Mexico. As the story goes, when Cortés landed in Veracruz, he gave the orders to his soldiers to burn the boats. Why? Because he was leaving them no choice but to succeed or die trying.

Some entrepreneurs believe the only way to win is to burn the proverbial boats, leaving winning as the only option. For example, we've all seen someone on social media boasting about "risking it all." They quit their jobs with no clients and no real sense of what their business will do but they're "going all in." They'll borrow against their house, cars or from family members, and if it doesn't work out, they'll lose everything.

They'll hire employees or sign up for something knowing they don't actually have the cash. And, for some, this approach has worked. While it's an approach I couldn't make sense of, I also couldn't ignore the incredible results it *appeared* to yield. What were they doing that I wasn't? Was it really all just a matter of luck?

"People prefer the certainty of misery over the misery of uncertainty."
—*Virginia Satir*

INTRODUCTION
TUG OF WAR

Are you a winner?

A question like this can make some people sit up a little straighter and exclaim, "You know it!" while others shy away from competition altogether.

If you're an entrepreneur, you might not *think* you're in a game of sorts, but you are. For most of us who have entered the world of business, we all want to win—even if we don't deem ourselves competitive.

Every day, month or year can be reviewed as a win or loss, and for those who have endured the absolute struggles of running a business, working in one, losing one or being fired, you know it can often feel like gambling: exciting but unpredictable.

Years ago, I started to analyze how others were winning this game of entrepreneurship. Was there seriously some mathematical formula where *success in business = good fortune + positive mindset + X*?

As I am naturally mathematically inclined, I like plugging variables into a formula and getting an answer. I like to know that if I do X and Y, then Z will happen.

But I also know life is inherently filled with dynamic complexities. A formula is therefore not a realistic way of looking at the world. All-or-nothing thinking and sweeping generalizations are things I actively try to avoid. And with those states of mind ruled out, I found the answer I was looking for— and I hated it.

So what's the secret to business success?

It depends.

Seems vague, right? Vague and so very frustrating.

What exactly does "it" depend on?

Very simple: You.

What you do, the actions that you take and the decisions that you make depend entirely on *what you want.*

That's it.

You, specifically, might want to grow your business by 50 percent in the coming years. Someone else of the same age, with the same number of kids, running the same type of business, might want to keep revenue the same as last year. And guess what?

Both of you would be correct.

You might want to spend more time with your family while someone else might want to build a rocket to Mars.

Again, both would be correct.

However, each of these paths is based on different needs, which means they will require unique strategies.

This kind of dynamic complexity is frightening and confusing for most of us. Society promotes one version of success and what it yields—the mansions, the cars, the seven-figure businesses. But, of course, not all of us actually want this. There's no single blueprint to run a successful business.

The problem is that most of us don't take time to define what success looks like to us in the first place.

Instead, we swallow whole the narrative that we should

idolize entrepreneurs. We call them changemakers, seekers and disruptors who change the world. We see the influencer pages of successful entrepreneurs with millions of followers, endless accolades, TED Talks and billion-dollar exits and think:

Should I be doing that?

Whatever the reasoning behind some of this world's greatest successes, it's in our nature to want success in some capacity. For some, the fulfillment is in creating something from scratch and building a legacy to be proud of. For others, it's giving back to the underserved community. To create our own product or company we can be proud of. To take care of our family. To buy the shiny car. Most of us want to hit the coveted benchmark of making enough money so that we don't feel stuck.

Regardless of what it is you really want, it feels like some seem to win, no matter what the circumstance or business, while others seem to stumble and fall. And if you happen to be new to the game of entrepreneurship, you might be uncertain about how to proceed, desperate to know the secrets of those successful men and women who've come before you. You don't want to be the one to stumble. You don't want to fail. You want to skip all the mistakes and just get to the good part.

But here's the thing:

Everyone stumbles.
Everyone fails.
Everyone has doubts. And yet, *you can still win.*

The answer is to clearly define what winning looks like for you.

Oftentimes, it's easier to admire—even covet—someone else's success than it is to clearly define and strive for our own. Most of us know someone whose track record in business seems to get better and better as they pile up countless wins. Let's call this guy Gary. Try as you might, you can't put your finger on why Gary sees so much consistent success while you struggle aimlessly from business to business, thinking that this time will bring the winning formula. Meanwhile, Gary's thriving and you're flailing.

Instead of digging deeper into your own process or systems, you're focused on Gary. What's Gary doing? How has Gary seemed to rig the game in his favor so that he *wins all the time and never strikes out and never makes a mistake no matter how close anyone is watching?*

Does Gary just have amazing business acumen, a deeper knowledge of entrepreneurship, a better handle on money, the proper growth strategy, a killer team or an *annoyingly* positive mindset that makes him a resilient freak of nature? Is Gary performing some sort of magical voodoo spell that works on everyone but you?

You begin to resent Gary. Gary is a threat to your success, and you start to wonder what the point of it all is if Gary is out there doing it bigger and better than you in the first place.

Screw you, Gary!

Here's the thing: It's not magic that Gary's got. It's an *operating system*—a really effective operating system that can be examined and even replicated.

Whether you're a veteran entrepreneur like Gary or a brand-new business owner just learning the ropes, chances are you've got a list a mile long of concerns, to-do goals, Key Performance Indicators (KPIs) and systems in place. And the one thing you have in common with Gary—and even Bill Gates and the Kardashians, believe it or not—is that in the beginning of building a business or a brand, there is financial uncertainty.

While you don't have to be an entrepreneur to face financial uncertainty, when the success of your company rests directly on your shoulders, the stakes are higher. Everything becomes uncertain because you can't predict what's coming: your next paycheck, your next client, your next team member who suddenly quits.

Or can you?

This feeling of uncertainty comes from a mix of anxiety and powerlessness, and it's compounded by a tendency to make analytical decisions instead of tuning into things we *actually* value.

The best part? This uncertainty is fixable—no, it's preventable, which is exactly what we're going to discover in this book.

Why should you trust me? The short answer is that I've finally learned to trust myself. As an Accounting and E-Commerce Information Systems graduate, I was selected out of a pool of nominees from the nation's top 50 accounting programs for an exclusive fellowship with the Governmental Accounting Standards Board (GASB), where I helped write a national accounting standard. Since then, I've worked in finance, tax and accounting roles at Deloitte and other Fortune 500 companies. I won awards, was named to elite lists and rose in the ranks as the textbook example of a "successful career in business"...and I was miserable. I had been working full-time since I was in college, and the intensity increased in my early post-graduate life. I thought: *Could this corporate drudgery really be the endgame?* Thankfully, it wasn't.

When I finally became a full-time entrepreneur, I unknowingly had to unlearn a lot of things. It wasn't a smooth transition, and I experienced the type of failure most entrepreneurs face. Some push through; others quit. I'm a problem solver by nature, so I took each blow as a challenge. In the process, I had the privilege of advising thousands of clients, launching two seven-figure businesses, leading a successful software project and learning from countless investments—and in the process, I learned what works and what doesn't.

All that's code for: I'm really good at teaching others how to streamline their businesses, increase revenue and not lose their souls in the process (I promise).

I created *Rigging the Game* for people just like you because I used to be just like you. This easy-to-navigate, step-by-step operating system helps you achieve and sustain financial certainty in your own entrepreneurship game so you don't have to second-guess what you're not doing—or rely on luck.

Rigging the Game will lay out the top three reasons why some people seem to win all the time while others don't; the Four Commandments for achieving financial certainty; the proprietary algorithms to make your new Operating System work; and the proper steps to identifying priorities and fully funding them in an ideal timeline.

This methodology includes:

→ How to identify personal biases and evolve past limiting binary thinking
→ Actionable steps for turning goals into accessible checkpoints and allocating assets accordingly
→ Useful decision-making frameworks
→ Recapturing and reallocating resources to get closer to what you want

While there's always going to be inherent risk in business, this book will teach you how to troubleshoot the most common mistakes to rig the game in your favor.

If you want to build a system that is "rigged" or rather one that produces the outcomes you want, the most efficient first step is to compile and analyze the systems that already work. Not just for you, but for everybody.

And since this book is ultimately about purpose-driven

entrepreneurs—business leaders and what *they* want rather than the business itself and what *it* wants—then you should study what other successful entrepreneurs are doing as a proxy. And then we're going to build upon it and create a model designed specifically for *you*.

Once you understand the Commandments and Operating System, you must apply them to the "it depends" scenario. You do this by defining who you are (what I call your style of play) and what you want (what I refer to as The Solvable Problem™, where you define your style, assign assets and determine gaps).

Everything I'm going to present here has been collected and distilled from more than 3,000 conversations with clients, mentors, friends, connections and my own experiences and insight from a decade of owning and operating my own companies. And much to my surprise, despite the different desires or outcomes, I've realized that every single business owner is facing the same universal problem.

And it's the same problem I've been asked to solve throughout my career, the question I've been asked to answer over and over again and it goes something like this:

"Am I going to be okay?"

Which really translates to: "Am I going to run out of cash?"

In other words, while everyone's priorities are different, they are all looking for the same damn thing: *certainty*.

Certainty that they will be able to fully fund the things that matter to them and do so in a timeline that is appropriate for their needs.

Certainty that they can fulfill their dreams on their timeline.

Certainty that they can feed their families, pay their bills and take care of their staff.

Certainty that they will survive and hopefully thrive.

As I was struggling to articulate this idea, I came across an equation from entrepreneur and author Chip Conley that helped me make sense of how to solve the problem for myself, my partners and my clients. It was one of those "aha" moments —I remember exactly where I was and how I felt when it hit me. Conley's equation looks like this:

$$Anxiety = Uncertainty \times Powerlessness$$

Notice that it's multiplicative instead of additive, meaning that uncertainty and powerlessness *amplify* each other exponentially; a tiny increase in uncertainty and a tiny increase in the feeling of powerlessness will compound into massive amounts of anxiety.

My inner math geek spoke to me and told me that, according to the distributive property, I could add a single word to the equation and it would still hold true. The equation became:

$$\underline{Financial} \ Anxiety = \underline{Financial} \ Uncertainty \times \underline{Financial} \ Powerlessness$$

I don't know a single business owner who hasn't experienced this kind of anxiety. The good news? I've been able to distill the factors that *cause* the anxiety into an equation that can be solved with sound mathematical principles.

Once you have the context behind the success you want to model and the necessary mental framing and action steps to implement it in your own business, the mystery surrounding financial certainty and risk reduction becomes a lot less intimidating and frightening and instead becomes something you can feasibly conquer.

You don't have to be another failing statistic. You can rise above. You can be better. You can win. And while I want you to get revved up for what's ahead, I also want you to remember one very important fact: *There is no one way to win.* Success or "winning" is not that binary. Rather, the systems we will discuss are intended to get you closer to what you want without becoming someone else. Not even someone like Gary.

So if you're ready to rig the game in your favor, let's close the gap and open the door to possibility.

"Great spirits have always encountered violent opposition from mediocre minds."
—*Albert Einstein*

PART I

THREE REASONS WHY SOME PEOPLE ALWAYS WIN (WHILE OTHERS DON'T)

IDENTIFY YOUR BIASES

S uccessful people *don't* necessarily win all the time—and what we tend to label "good luck" is actually just preparedness for the known unknowns; put another way, they have rigged the game for the unknown. And people who can acknowledge the existence of known unknowns, not to mention doing the work to understand the nature of that very principle, are the ones who seem to have all the luck. The rest of us are stuck with the "unlucky breaks" because we simply aren't prepared.

A simple fix for this? *Stop violating your own economic and personal principles.*

Obvious? Maybe. But humans come pre-wired with biases that make it nearly impossible to recognize when we are setting ourselves up for defeat. For example, take how Nobel Memorial Prize-winning psychologist Daniel Kahneman laid out this principle in his book, *Thinking Fast and Slow*:

A. A woman has bought two $20 tickets to the theater. When she arrives at the theater, she opens her wallet and discovers that the tickets are missing but $20 tickets are still available at the box office. Will she buy two more tickets to see the play?

B. A woman goes to the theater, intending to buy two tickets that cost $20 each. She arrives at the theater, opens her wallet and discovers, to her dismay, that the $40 with which she was going to make the purchase fell out of her pocket somewhere on the street. Tickets for $20 are still available at the box office. She has a credit card. Will she buy the tickets and just charge them?

In the first scenario, where the tickets were purchased but missing, most people believe that she would go home without buying another ticket and say that they would do the same.

In the second scenario, where she lost the cash, most people assume she would buy a ticket and say they would do the same.

This is an example of the mental accounting bias. The scenarios are identical: Would this woman pay $80 to go to the show or not? The fact that most people would make one decision in scenario A and a different decision in scenario B means that in one case, they are violating their own economic and personal principles because of the *way* the problem was presented.

While we may be clear on our economic and personal principles in theory, we do not always act in accordance with those principles in reality because of how they are presented to us. Cognitive biases like the recency bias, anchoring bias and mental accounting bias sometimes cause us to act in direct opposition to our values.

Being aware of these biases is not enough to protect us against them, however. The G.I. Joe fallacy, coined by Laurie Santos and Tamar Gendler of Yale University, states that knowing biases exist does not mean we will recognize or be able to avoid them in real time. We need to have systems in place to filter our actions so that we don't end up defeating ourselves.

While we are wired for biases, most design their systems to assume they are not subject to biases. Or that this time, they will try harder, as if trying harder is the simple solution to everything. (Spoiler alert: It's not).

Thinking Fast and Slow explores the two decision-making systems we use when confronted with problems, and before I go into the particulars of the systems themselves, I want to talk about what's led me to care about this in the first place.

I was on my fourth job after my accounting fellowship. And while it was still in the "finance" space, it was honestly my fourth complete career change and I was exhausted.

I was starting to realize that it wasn't the employers who were the problem—it was *me*. So I began seeking out resources for support—books, online programs and anything internet marketing threw at me. I found that every program I purchased started with "mindset" work from folks with zero formal training—potentially dangerous and irresponsible, in my opinion.

The prevailing comments from the conductors of these programs when clients weren't getting the outcomes they wanted ran along the lines of this sentiment: "Fix your mindset."

It seemed to me like nothing more than a convenient excuse for their lack of performance. You see, in most master classes, there's a very convenient way that coaches tell you you're not getting the results you want: You have mindset issues. While that may be true in some cases, there's no way to customize a program to each person's mindset, what I call the Solvable Problem™. It's just: There's one way to do this, and if you don't, you lose.

No thanks.

That's when I started to question whether mindset was actually enough. Because if mindset was enough—and I had done years of work on my mindset, by this point—then why did I still have such huge *holes* in my decision-making? The initial explanation could still be, "'Cause you need to fix your mindset, bro!" But that just didn't make sense to me as the exclusive answer. And when something "just doesn't make sense," I can't let it lie.

These mindset approaches don't take into account our bias, and that is a critical flaw. Without addressing everyone's individual bias and building a system that assumes everyone will operate at their peak, it's destined to fail. That would be like a marathon runner assuming that every day they would hit a personal record. We know that's not the case. It's better to build a system where you can run consistently at an average pace. And when you run faster, it's a bonus—but not the expectation.

Not only does this approach set you up to win—and even overachieve—it allows you to let go of the shame and guilt of not achieving perfection every time.

So as I re-approached my journey into understanding the mindset, I dove into trying to understand the ways in which we, as brain-having humans, process decisions and how we might improve the results of those processes once we have a handle on them (which led me to Kahneman's explanation of our two systems).

These two systems revolve around The Human Mindset and The Champion's Mind.

The Human Mindset is Kahneman's System 1 and establishes that without a system or solid framework to make decisions, you will lean heavily on your hardwired biases. As Dr. Jeff Spencer says, "There's a reason why it's called 'mindset': the mind is set." In other words, the human mindset is fixed. Intuitively that makes sense, as the human mindset is oriented toward survival. It allows us to act and react with minimal energy, which is the reason it gets "first dibs." The Human Mindset is that quick-thinking, impulsive part of our brain, which means it's at the mercy of our biases. When we're feeling competitive, defensive or experiencing FOMO, this mindset kicks in. As you can imagine, it presents a dangerous roadblock for forward progress.

The Champion's Mind is Kahneman's System 2 and is oriented toward success. The Champion's Mind is not set or fixed. While a select few seem to come naturally inclined to adopt the Champion's Mind, it's not a birthright. It can be honed with intentional practice, and while it doesn't have first dibs, it does have the final say if we have the tools to put it to work when necessary.

System 1 is our automatic, intuitive and unconscious mode. Dr. Jordan Poppenk, Canada Research Chair in Cognitive Neuroscience, found that we have an average of 6,200 thoughts per day.

For example, think about recording a Zoom video for your team or your clients—you may be moving your hands around, trying to project your voice, making sure you have the right posture, remembering to look at the camera and wondering what your audience is or isn't doing. These are all things that require independent thoughts and happen very, very quickly.

If you go out to grab lunch later, perhaps you've got to cross the street and thus make sure you don't get hit by a car. There are a lot of things to navigate. You're making thousands of micro-decisions. You don't *consciously* think about moving your right leg and then your left leg; you're just walking. And if a car comes, you instinctively look around, stop and get out of the way.

So that's System 1 in the context of Daniel Kahneman's research and it represents this idea that part of our brain has to move really, really fast because we have to make all of these micro-decisions. Think about it: We couldn't survive if we had to take the time to think, *Now I'm going to move my right leg, then my left leg.* We wouldn't be able to exist in the modern world with that awareness of thought. Instead, we have to be able to make these really quick actions with really quick thoughts—and this system is subject to biases.

On the other hand, System 2 is the slow, controlled, analytical and thoughtful method where logic and reason dominate. It's the slow-plotting part of our brain, the part we use when working through a math equation, putting together an Excel workbook or, if you're a nerd like me, analyzing the tax code. It's the part of your brain you use to build out a marketing funnel. You have to really plot through these things, pause and ask yourself about the outcome that you want. What are you trying to get to and why?

That's the part of our brain that operates in System 2. It's very conscious, we're aware of it and this system is what I believe can be optimized through mindset work.

That work, if we want it to be effective, begins with a thorough understanding of not only *how* our brains make decisions —as in the systems we just covered—but an awareness of the biases that influence us and how we might recognize and minimize the impact of those biases on our judgment.

HUMAN NATURE MENTALITIES	
HUMAN MINDSET	**CHAMPION'S MIND™**
What do I stand to lose?	What do I stand to gain?
I'm doing my best	I'll find a way
It's in my genes	It's in my power
If I were only like others	I'm my greatest asset
Will and talent are enough	Discipline and readiness rule
It's about perfection	It's the 1-2 things that count
I'm afraid so won't even try	I trust and just do it
I whine	I win

As I said before, in System 1, The Human Mindset gets first dibs. Before we react or go with our gut, we have to create some space to allow the Champion's Mind the opportunity to have a say. In the words of Viktor Frankl, Holocaust survivor, neurologist and psychologist: "Between stimulus and response, there is a space. In that space is our power to choose our response. In our response lies our growth and freedom."

If we can create the cognitive space, then we give ourselves the opportunity to choose: Do we allow the Human Mindset to dictate the terms or will we harness the Champion's Mind?

There are many tools out there for creating space such as journaling and meditation. The distinction I would bring to you, however, is that we must identify the patterns in our thinking so we can create the framework first. These patterns are often cognitive distortions or unhelpful thinking styles that can cause us to beat ourselves at our own game.

Let's say you've achieved a seven-figure business and then no longer have a seven-figure business. But you've anchored yourself to the idea that you *have* a seven-figure business and now you need to take every action to avoid the loss of having to say that you don't actually have a seven-figure business. This is an expression of the anchoring bias or the cognitive bias, which causes us to rely on the very first piece of information we're given about a topic.

The flaw in this line of thinking is that you've anchored yourself to something that wasn't true and now you're trying to avoid losing something that didn't exist to begin with.

If we fail to identify our biases, like the loss aversion and anchoring biases in this example, we may begin to make decisions that take us further from what we actually want in the name of maintaining something we never had, which, in this case, is a seven-figure business.

This is why we have to take inventory of our biases and have real clarity around us so we can avoid anchoring ourselves to a false narrative, which is also a type of bias.

When we talk about identifying our biases in decision-making, it's important to distinguish between individual indexing and group indexing. Indexing, at its most basic, is a way of sorting data into categories (most commonly into a database or table for later use). Data that is indexed, whether by a person, a computer or a machine of some sort, is meant to be used to make a reliable, accurate decision.

Individual indexing is a measurement of factors specific to you. To use a personal health example, individual indexing would be the Fitbit or Oura Ring you wear that tells you your specific heart rate, sleep patterns, breathing, what time you get up and when you go to bed. These are data points that pertain to you and you alone, and they can be used to reliably make decisions regarding your health and habits.

Group indexing, on the other hand, is based on averages. You're likely pretty similar to the *average* example of someone in your demographic for age, height, weight and the area in which you live. Based on these demographics, we could make assumptions about things that might be true for you to make decisions. But you wouldn't want your doctor to prescribe a treatment for you based on what the average example of your demographic needs. You want your treatment plan customized to *you* and your individual needs.

So bringing that concept back around to the topic of identifying our biases, you'll want to create a personal index of biases that you personally are prone to so that you can reliably identify them. This isn't necessarily to eliminate them because that's not realistic. But you can build those biases into the systems you use to make decisions so that those systems are perfectly designed to generate the outcome that serves you and your priorities best.

Yo-yo dieting and budgeting are good examples of this type of thinking. We build a system assuming we will operate at an extreme—*Never going to eat carbs again! Not buying Starbucks* *anymore because it'll save me $7 per day!*—and then wonder why it explodes.

Consider looking at things from a perspective of relative change—a fraction that describes the size of the absolute change in comparison to the reference value. Any time you go from zero to one, the relative change is undefined. But we try to build a system where the change is zero to 1,000.

So unless you have the unique disposition to maintain extremes in perpetuity (it's prudent to assume less than .1 percent do), it's better to build the system assuming that you are subject to biases. Then, if you aren't subject to any biases, that just creates an additional upside.

Let's look at the performance of traders. Most of us have a strong sense of loss aversion. If our stock goes down, then we don't want to sell because we lock in a loss. But the top traders are generally quick to lock in losses because they know another investment will make their money back faster.

The repeat winners have identified the biases most likely to knock them off track and have built systems to prevent this from happening in the first place.

Cognitive Distortions: Unhelpful Thinking Habits

Five years ago, I bought another business to bolt on to an existing client base. At the risk of being hyperbolic, it turned into the biggest disaster of my career. I considered selling the firm and doing something entirely different. For months, I would ruminate over how I got there. I thought I did all of the research before I made my move and yet, by my definition of success, it was a complete failure.

So I took a step back and hired the top Ph.D. I could find in the Seattle area who specialized in anxiety. He gave me a copy of Dr. David D. Burns' book *The Feeling Good Handbook* and an accompanying worksheet, and that's where I learned about cognitive distortions. The following 10 cognitive distortions did a world of good for me and I believe they'll do the same for you.

All-or-Nothing Thinking: *The tendency to evaluate your personal qualities or options in extreme, black-or-white categories.*

Overgeneralization: *The process of concluding (arbitrarily) that one thing that happened to you (or that you saw or heard about) once will occur over and over again.*

Mental Filter: *The process of picking out a negative detail in any situation and dwelling on it exclusively, thereby perceiving the whole situation as negative.*

Disqualifying the Positive: *Transforming neutral or even positive experiences into negative ones by filtering out positive information, dismissing it as a fluke, or convincing oneself that it "doesn't count."*

Jumping to Conclusions (Mind Reading, the Fortune Teller Error): *Arbitrarily jumping to a conclusion not supported by the facts.*

Magnification and Minimization (AKA the "Binocular Trick"): *Errors, fears and imperfections are exaggerated while strengths and achievements are made to seem small and unimportant.*

Emotional Reasoning: *In which emotions are taken as evidence of truth.*

"Should" Statements: *Attempts to motivate ourselves by saying, "I should do this" or "I must do that," leading to apathy and shame or self-loathing.*

Labeling and Mislabeling: *An extreme form of overgeneralization in which we label ourselves with oversimplified and usually negative attributes.*

Personalization and Blame: *Assuming responsibility for a negative even when there is no basis for doing so; concluding that what happened was your fault or reflects your inadequacy, even when you were not responsible for it.*

These cognitive distortions send people into self-sabotaging loops of doom every single day. But this isn't about you versus other people. It's about you versus you.

Rig the Game:

1. What are ways the human mindset controls you?
2. What are the cognitive distortions you're subject to?

2

PLAY YOUR OWN GAME

I'm a Seattle Seahawks fan, for better *and* for worse. (Yes, I know, run the ball on the one-yard line in the Super Bowl!) One of the most frustrating things about watching them play over the last decade is knowing that, while they are clearly talented enough to win, they continually make decisions that work against them. If you're a Seahawks fan, you know what I mean. At times when they should definitely be winning, they almost seem to beat *themselves*. From afar, it appears if they would just stop getting in their own way, or competing against themselves, they would consistently do much better.

Unfortunately, business owners work the same way—they are unknowingly beating themselves by trying to push harder on the gas without releasing the emergency brake. So it would seem that the easiest way to make faster progress without working harder is to simply release the brake, right?

The problem is that business owners and entrepreneurs are constantly surrounded by success stories—some of which seem to have the same name attached to them every single time. Remember Gary from the introduction? Yeah, we hate him.

With every success story Gary shares, he becomes really difficult to ignore.

Because we live in a comparison culture, we work harder to compete with Gary, pressing on that gas, not understanding how people like Gary continue to win constantly, especially after taking what seems like a lot of risks, while others (you) can't seem to catch the same kind of big break.

Since this book is all about rigging the game in your favor, let's look at people who figured out that business *is* a game in the first place. Think about all the wildly successful icons we know: Elon Musk, Oprah Winfrey, Aliko Dangote, Jeff Bezos, Bill Gates, Patrice Motsepe; even rock stars like Mick Jagger or the late great David Bowie. (And let's not forget Gary!)

What are these icons known for *other* than their success? We know them for setting their own rules and not playing anyone else's game. Do you think Oprah decided to twiddle her thumbs and do as she was told until she hit her big break? Or that Elon Musk thought, *Hmm, I'll just change the world by doing things exactly as they've been done before?* No.

While I'm not saying you have to be an innovator or a larger-than-life leader, I am saying you have to figure out what makes you you *before* you find success.

Because that *is* your success.

Oprah found success in media because communication and connection are built into who she is. Bill Gates became a technology pioneer because he'd been inventing software since he was a teenager. Every success story you've heard about enigmatic leaders such as these is rooted in personal passion. Ask yourself: *What allows you to play your game?* In other words, express yourself for who you are before you were told you had to be someone else to "make it."

How can you possibly expect to generate outsized results by conforming to the behaviors of everyone around you? As Albert Einstein once said, "Insanity is doing the same thing over and over and expecting different results." That's effectively what we're doing when we act as a conformist while simultaneously expecting different outcomes.

Unknowingly, we're making one of two arguments.

Argument one is that we'll just outwork everyone else. In other words, we're arguing that success is really a function of effort and time. There is evidence to suggest that by working 10,000 hours, we can become domain experts. Great! But I've yet to find a causal relationship between effort and success. Effort doesn't necessarily cause you to be successful. Success and effort are merely related.

Argument two is one of exceptionalism. Exceptionalism is the belief that you, your society and your movement are inherently just better (exceptional) than everything and everyone else. The term inherently implies that you're superior in some or many ways. When you adopt the exceptionalism approach, you are permitting yourself to act like everyone else because your inherent superiority will cause you to succeed. If you're this far into this book, I'd imagine you know this is a bias and thus a framework that isn't serving you in advancing your goals.

I'm not advocating for being an annoyance to those around you by resisting the status quo. I'm not suggesting that you take the difficult path just for the sake of it. I'm saying you need to play your own game. In researching this book, I read a lot about extraordinary leaders and there was no single data point that correlated success with being agreeable. In fact, the consequence of playing your game is that you end up saying "no" a lot.

If you're a people pleaser, which many of us are, the idea of saying "no" is cause for extreme anxiety. What we fail to understand however is that being agreeable and saying "yes" to every request is actually saying "no" to other possibilities. Time and money are scarce resources. "No" can actually allow for more opportunities to grow—and to win.

Let me give a few examples of other consequences of failing to play your game.

Let's say you get to the championship game, but then you lose because you were playing someone else's style (the Seahawks being a run-first team that loses the Super Bowl because they threw the ball). That's a much bigger pill to swallow than losing, but you stuck to your principles.

Conversely, say you're a coach and you're constantly losing because your team has no identity; week after week, you're trying to borrow from everyone else. That'll get you fired or your job will be unstable because you can't sustain yourself copying others.

There's a quote by Virginia Satir that says: "Most people prefer the certainty of misery to the misery of uncertainty." It's so powerful and disorienting that I started this book with it. But why do most of us prefer predictable misery to uneasy uncertainty? Because while we are all going on our own hero's journey, so many of us borrow versions of success or attempt to play someone else's game instead of our own.

It's convenient and overly simplistic to just tell someone to create a vision board and figure out their *why*, right? However, most people don't know their why, and when they're asked to figure it out, it causes them more anxiety and shame. It's like telling a depressed person that they'll be okay. While your intentions are good, you're dismissing how the person is really doing.

What's funny, however, is when we meet the eccentric billionaire, we often write off their eccentricities because, well, they are a billionaire. But here's the thing: We need to understand causation versus correlation. Being a billionaire didn't necessarily *cause* them to be eccentric. In fact, when you really study their bios, they were eccentric first. It likely wasn't socially acceptable then, but when they got billions, it became acceptable.

The point is that we don't have to conform to one way. The cognitive load is much too great to pretend to be someone else. It's a bit hyperbolic, but you would have to be a sociopath to yield consistent results over a long duration of time while playing someone else's game. It's a fragile and thus unsustainable construct.

There's a line from Lewis Carroll's *Alice's Adventures in Wonderland* that seems apropos of this discussion. The Mad Hatter says, "Am I going mad?" To which Alice replies, "Yes, you're mad, bonkers, off the top of your head...but...I'll tell you a secret. All the best people are."

Think about Elon Musk's tweets (or even the name of his child), Lady Gaga's self-expression through fashion (and sometimes meat) or that time Mick Jagger bought a multimillion-dollar mansion while in a questionable cognitive state and then jumped directly onto a horse, having never ridden one before.

If we let these seemingly odd habits define these moguls, we might write them off as weird or eccentric. Instead, these individuals attained the success they have *because* they have been playing their own game and no one else's since long before we even knew their names. They had unconventional ways of thinking and a stubborn refusal to conform. For the purposes of this topic, I should say that they identified their priorities and biases *early*, which has allowed them to march to the beat of their own drum since the beginning.

Do you march to the beat of your own drum? Do you capitalize on what makes you you? Do you follow your gut instincts when it comes to business decisions? The most successful business owners—rather, the ones who consistently get what they want—are the ones who make moves that bring them closer to what they prioritize rather than focusing on activities that maximize shareholder value or bring them more clients, resources or revenue.

They might seem different to the people who are focused

on what society has told them to because these rare individuals have established their own core set of values and behave in a way to get closer to what they want without getting knocked off course.

While some of us are born as we are and don't veer off course for even a second, some of us become entrenched in what society wants us to be. How our parents want us to live. What our bosses think our talent is worth. What Gary thinks we should do. We've all likely heard the statistics on how creativity diminishes as kids get older. That's because they learn to conform. Schools teach us "the right way," but most things in life come down to preference. It wasn't until I stopped trying to play other people's games that I unlocked my true potential. And you can, too.

So how do you figure out how to stay in your own lane, in a game built entirely for you? You have to go beyond saying who you are and take massive action. Success isn't made by thought alone. Unless you're a sociopath, how can you expect to consistently get results while acting like someone you're not?

To put it another way, how can you expect to be extraordinary while conforming to the strategies of the average? It's a fragile existence.

Luckily, there is a way to bridge that gap between who you say you are and what you do.

What someone *says* about themselves might be, "I have integrity, excellence and I care about about my relationships." And they genuinely believe these things are true. Conversely, values in action would be what they are actually doing.

My belief is that the gap between what you say about yourself and what you actually do represents the level of self-awareness that you have. So, if what you say about yourself and what you actually do are consistently in alignment and true to each other, then you probably have a high level of self-awareness. If there's a significant gap, then you have a low level of self-awareness.

I've discovered over the years that some of the smartest people—that is, the people with the most cognitive horsepower—struggle the most with these biases. Business owners who have committed to improving themselves and reaching their goals actually fight themselves the most, creating unnecessary friction. Ray Dalio discusses this in his book, *Principles For Dealing with the Changing World Order*. Or look at the way Warren Buffett evaluates investments.

In order to achieve the success that they have, these business owners had to adopt a paradigm, a set of assumptions that allowed them to play at the highest level possible without thinking through every little detail. However, unlike you (since you're reading this right now), they are unaware of the theories or assumptions they have adopted—and even the fact that they are using them at all. Remember that the system is perfectly designed to create the outcomes you want. In order to get the outcomes you want, you have to understand how the system works to either re-engineer it or change the inputs.

Counterintuitively, we learn in Chris Argyris's Harvard Business Review article "Teaching Smart People How to Learn" the paradoxical quality of high-performance humans creates the biggest obstacle to lasting success: The values people think are driving them are not the values or principles they actually use in their everyday lives.

We can learn to recognize the gap between our espoused values and values in action by designing and implementing *our own actions* (playing our own game). With a sound operating system like the one I'm going to teach you in this book, and a little bit of awareness, you can start to recognize the inconsistencies in your behavior and put our espoused values to the test.

In order to stop playing against ourselves or getting in our own way, your espoused values and values in action must be aligned.

When they are, we will always play by our own rules.

Rig the Game:

1. In what ways do you observe that you tend to conform to norms versus lean into your unique disposition?
2. If you could play your own game with no limitations, what would you do differently?

3

CARRY A TOOLKIT

There are a million podcasts and books covering the tools and tricks of the successful. Some meditate, some are early risers, some are stoics, some post incessantly on Instagram and some are even named Gary.

There's a tendency to mirror the practices of those whom you admire. Say you're a super fan of former Navy SEAL Commander Jocko Willink. One day, you're scrolling through *Business Insider* and you spot the article written by Richard Feloni published on November 20, 2017, "A day in the life of a retired Navy SEAL commander, who wakes up at 4:30 am, trains in Brazilian jiujitsu and doesn't eat for 72 hours at a time."

You read through the article with zeal and you learn that Jocko:

1. Wakes up at 4:30 am Monday through Sunday (in other words, every day)
2. Starts each day with about an hour of lifting weights, plus cardio

3. Doesn't eat breakfast, but eats lunch between 11 am and noon
4. Eats dinner at 8pm, which typically includes steak and vegetables
5. Goes to bed at 11pm

You want to be like Jocko, so you copy the schedule. And what happens? You start to see results, but they're not sustainable for you because you need more than 5.5 hours of sleep and you hate vegetables. Why does this work so well for Jocko but not for you?

First, you weren't playing *your* game. Second, you applied tools that weren't calibrated to your tendencies.

So what are we to make of this? It'd be easy to think: *Let me pick the person I want to be like and just copy them.* That would, however, violate playing our own game (see Chapter 2).

Instead, we should take from it not that we should copy their toolkit, but rather we *need to create our own toolkit.* Let's circle back to the Jocko example. What we did was attempt to mirror his life—and failed. But there's an alternative.

Rather than copy the plan line by line because we align with his edict that "discipline equals freedom," we can extract something much greater: Jocko has a system that works for *him.*

But you have to find the system that works for you. Now, for most people, that means trying to come up with something wildly different or new. Some new tool or strategy that we've never heard of before. Some guru that's selling an entirely new way to do business without stress. But the greats know that's not a winning strategy.

Consider Quincy Jones, who realized that to master music, one should endeavor to know everything that has been done within 12 notes—or Sun Tzu, who reiterates that point by explaining that there are only five primary colors that, in combination, produce more hues than imaginable.

Their secret is simply what's true: Every tool you need already exists.

It's how we modify or combine those tools that creates something unique to *us*. But, we are all starting with the same base set of options. Jocko doesn't have a different set of tools than Quincy, Oprah or even Gary.

We're all pulling from the same well. The trick is to figure out what your tools are trying to accomplish. We know they need to:

- Get us closer to what we want
- Decipher preference versus binary
- Drive home that every decision is a financial decision

By overcoming our initial biases, we can decide how to get "closer" faster, which means we need tools to help us get (and stay) in the right state of mind, process issues and properly evaluate growth.

Personally, I do a quarterly "archaeological dig" to figure out my gaps (some might call it a post-mortem) and then adjust accordingly. I go back over the decisions that I've made the past quarter to identify two things:

1. Decisions I made that did not get me closer to what I wanted
2. Why I made those decisions

For the first, I am trying to figure out where the gaps in my decision-making were. Was there some kind of bias I got caught up in? The challenge with biases is you think you know all of them, but many biases are ingrained and almost instinctual (repetitive behavior or patterns). Others are systemic and can seem invisible (sexism and racism built into the systems of education, politics, business—you name it). The bias itself can prevent you from seeing it. So taking stock is key.

When it comes to exploring *why* I made a decision, I really examine my motivations' biases. For example, I am at my grumpiest in January for a number of reasons. The main one is that everyone makes their New Year's resolutions. Because they have decided to change their life, they expect you to conform to these changes without asking if they fit into your own life and routine.

Employees will come back newly motivated by a resolution of "get a raise!" and ask for one. I am always here to support my teams' growth, but I do not like the arbitrary nature of requesting a promotion tied to a resolution. Everyone gets frustrated and no one moves closer to what they want.

So I have a rule that I am not allowed to do anything new in January. This came out of a personal archaeological dig. I noticed a trend that I always felt this way in January and the actions I took often got me further away from what I wanted. It's that kind of self-discovery and reflection that can help refine anyone's principles and operating system.

This process is really aided by ongoing journaling and working with a coach who comes from a position of "it depends." This is why I created the Certified Certainty Advisor. I'm teaching other service providers all of this information to counterbalance the fake guru coaches who tell you there's only one way. In reality, they really just think that because they managed to climb to the top of Mt. Stupid (see the Dunning-Kruger effect)—and there's no way down.

So if you want to enjoy comparable success like Jocko's, you'll need a new set of tools as well as the necessary frameworks with which to refine them. If we use a framework like *Extraordinary Minds* by Howard Gardner, for example, we would see that there are trends within the categories of masters, makers, introspectors and influencers. Even within each of those categories, there's no *one way*. But we do need to find one because, as we've established, we're subject to biases, which means we may try to solve the same problem differently every time because we're not able to glean that it's a problem we've already faced before.

And so the cycle continues.

People who seem to win constantly aren't better than you. Yes, they have identified their biases and play by their own rules, but they are also using a different toolbox than you are. And beyond using different tools, these people are committed to continually refining those tools to serve them better and better over time.

Luckily, I have discovered a small business/purpose-driven entrepreneur toolbox that can help any purpose-driven entrepreneurs diagnose and solve the problems they run into. The toolbox consists of 12 tools bucketed into the following three categories:

1. Four frames from which you should view every single problem that will help you identify risks and know when to invest or divest from a particular thing
2. Four issue processors that will help you determine the most efficient path forward at any given moment
3. Four growth principles that will ensure that you do not blow yourself up by not being able to see around corners

You should view these tools as the start of your journey. Each frame, issue processor and growth principle should be adapted to your unique situation and disposition.

Further, I didn't set out to create 12 tools. It started with one. And, as math works, it went to two. And then three. Okay, you get the point. One by one, I developed these tools so that I wouldn't solve the same problem in a different way.

As you begin to implement these tools, you'll find new ones to add. And perhaps you'll even replace some of the tools I suggest with new versions of your own. Good job, you! If you can successfully adopt and implement these frameworks to evaluate your decisions, filter your ideas, prepare for unforeseen outcomes and keep your highest priorities at the center of your roadmap (so to speak), you'll be able to join the ranks of the "lucky ones" (looking at you, Gary) who continually rack up win after win after win—and they will be wins that come with a meaningful impact on the important parts of both your life and your business.

A confidence-boosting note here: You do not need to know *everything* about business.

No one actually does, and your lack of omniscience will not automatically consign you to the "unlucky" category of unprepared entrepreneurs.

Rig the Game:

1. What are the systems and processes you use to make decisions?
2. Are these systems and processes consistently applied? Why or why not?

"If you are always trying to be normal, you will never know how amazing you can be."
—Maya Angelou

PART II

THE CERTAINTY COMMANDMENTS

4

THE MINDSET FOR FINANCIAL CERTAINTY

A s we've now established, there are three reasons why some people always win and you don't (yet). They have identified their biases, they understand how to play their own game and they have created and frequently access their own unique toolkit.

Now, you may be thinking, *Cool, so what does that mean for me?*

I'm glad you asked.

As you likely observed, the three reasons why some people always win are all interrelated. That means we need to construct an integrated system that's dynamic enough to account for our unique disposition, our ever-evolving wants and desires and our blind spots (biases).

To build a working system, we must tell it what we want it to accomplish. And for that system to work, we need a new orientation. That orientation is toward the least amount of effort, the least amount of risk and the most amount of optionality.

This is in direct opposition to what we've been taught. We've been told that we need to amplify everything, to hustle, grind and go all in. Those teachings cause us to put in maximum effort, which often leads to a lot of shame and guilt when we still don't end up living the life we wanted.

We have also been told that we should burn the boats, bet on our ourselves and work tirelessly. And constantly. Those teachings are causing us to take maximum risk when we don't have the tools to fully assess the potential returns—and if the trade-offs are worth it.

The consequences of maximum effort and maximum risk is that we are left with no options. We've backed ourselves into a corner where now everything has to work or we are doomed. Nefariously, that causes us to double down on effort and risk. Which, again, leads to fewer options. See the pattern here?

This "traditional" framework leads to a dynamic where we've built systems and expectations that assume we will operate at our peak every day (like that endurance athlete expecting to set a new record with every workout).

This orientation leads to an incredibly fragile system. Any day we're not operating at our highest possible output is a day that we're not achieving our goals. That then often leads to feeling more anxiety, shame and guilt.

Flipping our orientation to the least amount of effort, least amount of risk and the most amount of options is simple—but it won't be easy.

When I ask a group of clients, business leaders and peers to identify as problem-solvers, most of the time, the entire group raises their hands. Therein lies a challenge. Many of us who have our identity tied up in problem-solving tend to unknowingly create our own problems just so that we have something to solve, which puts us back in the orientation of the most amount of effort.

A recent vacation I took provides a good example of this. My family was staying at a resort that had a strict policy for reserving pool chairs. They were first-come, first-served, which seems fair, but the rules also explicitly stated that one couldn't reserve a chair until 7 am each morning, and once claimed, the chair had to be "active" every hour or it would be released and given to someone else. There were two responses to this policy: Some people woke up early every morning to reserve their seats and spent a lot of time policing their chairs, and others enjoyed their vacations.

The problem-solvers were the first group. They were so intent on achieving the goal of reserving pool chairs that they gave up time to sleep in, relax and simply enjoy themselves. They exerted the most amount of effort and still did not get closer to what they wanted, unless their idea of an ideal vacation resembles the stress and rigidity of the workweek.

We don't want to live an existence of constant anxiety. Remember, anxiety = uncertainty x powerlessness. So to reduce anxiety, we must increase certainty and reduce powerlessness.

Certainty is a nebulous term because it's an infinite game. Just when we think we know what we want, life changes on us. It's easy to get caught up in trying to "get it right." That is, trying to construct exactly what you want now and forever. That creates a fragile system. Instead, we need to acknowledge that what we want will change and create a system dynamic enough to adapt.

The declaration I make about certainty is that I have created certainty when I have funded what I want, on my own terms and timeline, while accepting that it will change when presented with new information. To do this we must create a Solvable Problem™, which I discuss in detail in Chapter 14.

To address the powerlessness we feel when we're anxious, we need tools that also acknowledge that we are biased and, perhaps most importantly, we must declare that we are not willing to compromise on our identity. This is what I call playing your game. Remember those eccentric billionaires I discussed earlier? They were eccentric before they were rich and we need to acknowledge that we are going to play to our unique abilities and stop trying to conform to the average.

Without establishing clear desired outcomes and the parameters to operate within them, the outcomes would be random and unpredictable. Disastrously, you'd run the risk of the system optimizing for the wrong things.

All too often, I see business owners doing exactly that—unknowingly optimizing for the wrong things. At the root of this is a lack of base assumptions to reference under all conditions.

As Kevin Ashton, creator of the Internet of Things, says in his masterful book *How to Fly a Horse: The Secret History of Creation, Invention, and Discovery*, "The greatest test of your expertise is how explicitly you understand your assumptions."

Now, in this case, I'm going to replace "assumptions" with commandments. Why? Because we are creating a clear distinction that we are not to violate them. Assumptions feel changeable, whereas commandments feel concrete. It would be sinful to violate a commandment.

I refer to them as The Four Commandments of Financial Certainty. Certainty is what we are in pursuit of, after all. We all seek the certainty that we will realize our unique definition of winning at life without compromising to be someone else.

These Commandments power the entire operational system, so we will regularly come back to them. In any situation we're faced with, we need to use our toolkit to determine whether or not we're about to violate our Commandments. If we can conclude with a reasonably high probability that we are not, then we are on the correct path toward financial certainty. If we can't conclude certainty or otherwise feel at risk, then it's cause for further time and evaluation because, as we established above, the downsides are grave when we violate the Commandments.

Each Commandment will be broken down, along with

examples of the biggest impact that breaking these Commandments may have on your cash flow as well as risk.

The Four Commandments of Financial Certainty:

1. **Closer Over More:** Every action we take needs to get us closer to what actually matters to us.
2. **Preference versus Binary:** We must be able to discern when there is and is not a right or wrong.
3. **Every Decision Has Infinite Trade-Offs:** We must be aware that when we make one decision, we remove an infinite number of other possibilities.
4. **Business Decisions Should Have Asymmetric Upside:** We must understand that resources are scarce. All bets must have significant upside with little to no downside.

In the following chapters, I will break down each Commandment and its impact on effort, risk and optionality so you can understand how it helps you achieve your new orientation.

5

CERTAINTY COMMANDMENT #1:

CLOSER OVER MORE

E*very action we take needs to get us closer to what actually matters.*

The default reaction of the human mindset is not satisfaction but instead a craving for more. We assume having more is the solution to everything. This leads us down some dark roads. We spend more as we make more. We make more and then take on more risk. The consequence of more risk is that then we have all this volatility (sleepless nights, upset employees, upset vendors and failed investments).

Instead of focusing on more, we need to get clear on what we *want*. Not what someone else wants because, remember, we aren't playing someone else's game. Remember to create a system that is optimized for your rolling average so anything above is a bonus. The orientation must be least amount of effort, least amount of risk and most amount of options.

To acknowledge a reality and to comfort you that you're not alone, getting clear on what you want can be anxiety-inducing. You will have to wrangle with your desire to default to "more." That shows up in the desire to have everything *now*. It also shows up in the fallacy that there is a right and wrong to what you want. I address this specific issue under Commandment #2.

You will also have to confront that when you define what success looks like to you, you're also defining failure. That is, if you don't reach your definition of success, you may deem yourself a failure. Because of loss aversion, most are unwilling to define failure.

To compound matters, when we do attempt to define what we want, it often creates even more anxiety. That's because what we've defined is a multi-variable equation. Sorry, here comes some math.

See, if you've ever tried to solve for x in an equation like $x + y + z = 10$, you know it's impossible. That's because this is a multi-variable equation.

This is the race we run against ourselves with the things we want. For example, if you say to your spouse, "I want to buy a car," they might flatly say "no." Without knowing your motivations for wanting to buy the car or theirs for saying "no," it's hard for either of you to solve this problem (in other words, make the right decision).

But let's say instead they humor you and request more information. When you simply requested to buy a car, you didn't provide them with a Solvable Problem™.

At the simplest level, assuming you're not Scrooge McDuck-wealthy, they don't know if you can afford this car purchase, yet. Who knows, maybe you want a collectible that'll cost $750,000. I'm not a car person so don't push me on specifics.

Anyhow, they might ask things like:

What kind of car?

How much does it cost?

When do you want to buy the car?

What are the interest rates?

Then they might ask whether you'll trade in your current car, put cash down, consider leasing and so on. In getting those answers, they have all the inputs they need to do the math and solve whether the request is possible.

When wants aren't clearly defined, we can't solve our own equation. With the necessary variables, we can solve how much we actually need to fund our priorities. And then, we must reckon with ourselves.

Dr. Jeff Spencer's number-one piece of advice for high performers is a single word: *restraint.* He explains that "the key word in the champion's vocabulary is restraint. We have our best day, our best week or our best month, and at that point we are at the highest risk of pushing just a little too far and blowing ourselves up."

All too often, an athlete, executive or entrepreneur has their best week, month or season ever and instead of settling into the new level of play, they try to push just a little bit harder when the best move is to recognize the progress and ride the wave. It seems counterintuitive to "ride the wave" instead of push harder, but it's often the difference between getting what you want and, as Dr. Spencer says, "blowing yourself up."

Allow me to put this concept in terms of a trip using Google Maps.

We all know how Maps works: You input where you are and where you want to go and Google gets you there using real-time data on factors like traffic, closures and accidents on your route.

Here's the problem with the way business owners approach this idea: They aren't really clear on where they are. Nor do they have much more clarity about where they want to be. But they're trying to go *somewhere*, right? Here's a recent example of why this is so important:

A client came to me and said, "I need to make enough to pay someone else to do these tasks so I can get 10 hours a week back to think and spend with my family."

So we did a quick exercise to figure out how much more he would need: I asked a ton of questions and found out that this person was willing to pay $10,000 a month extra for salary with a little bit of wiggle room. I kept asking questions and discovered that this person was driving 55 minutes each way, six days a week to the office. This may seem unimportant, but watch how we turn this into a "closer" problem instead of a "more" problem:

I told them, "Alright, an office space five minutes from your house is $2,500 a month. So there are 10 hours of your time back in just drive time. So now you have your time back and only $2,500 to cover."

Boom.

Next, I suggested he go through his bank statements—business and personal—and cancel every single recurring payment he could live without. I told him he could add them back in later if necessary.

This approach is what I call the Two Oreo Principle. A few years back, I was self-reflecting on how I gained 10 pounds. What I realized was after moving to a new house, I started raiding my wife's snack cabinet. That amounted to me adding on average two Oreos a day to my diet. See, day to day, I didn't think much of eating two Oreos. I mean, it's only two. However, each Double Stuf Oreo has 70 calories. And if you eat two a day for a year, that's 51,100 calories or *14.6 pounds*. There was the weight.

Our financials are littered with scenarios like this: small transactions that on the surface don't seem like much but over a longer duration of time add up to a lot. So the Two Oreo Principle is just a fun way to describe compound interest.

I encourage my clients to at least do a quarterly review and look for their two Oreos.

For the person looking to get 10 hours back, the Two Oreo review resulted in:

- Gaining back 10 hours a week

- Eliminating $3,200+ in recurring expenses and subscriptions
- Getting time back without having to do more work or invest more time

Makes sense, no?

This is the difference between focusing on "more" being the answer and focusing on getting "closer" to what actually matters to you.

Unless you happen to run a massive corporation, your resources are limited, and driving around in circles is a waste of time, money, energy, bandwidth and just about everything else.

To make sure your trip actually lands you somewhere you want to be, you'll need to input an end destination. In non-metaphor speak, you need to get your priorities set. After that, it's a matter of making sure every decision you make or course of action you follow will get you closer and closer to the things you want.

Those who are consistently winning, the eccentric billion-aire types we discussed earlier, often seem different because they have clarity on what they want and are not afraid to pursue it; in other words, they act in a way that gets them closer to what they want while the rest of the world is focused on more.

Impact on Effort: High Month Paradigm

A few months before writing this book, a client of mine scheduled a call to celebrate their highest revenue year ever, about $60 million, and to plan the next moves since they had all this extra revenue. Much to their chagrin, it took about 45 minutes to discover that even though they had a record year and growing revenue, they were in the worst cash position they had *ever* been in. You can imagine their surprise. Though they were shocked, I wasn't. This is actually what I have come to expect.

As businesses grow, the periods that feel like prosperity can actually take you farther away from your priorities.

This is a concept I call the High Month Paradigm. This concept has to do with businesses that are growing as planned. Revenues are climbing, owners are happy and the business crests its highest month, financially speaking. Unfortunately, amid the joy at how well the organization is growing, the risk of bad things happening is also increasing. And those "bad things" often show up in sleepless nights for you, constant metaphorical fire drills and a slew of other issues that begin to pull you away from the goals you want to reach. All this because you haven't yet identified the risks that exist in your business.

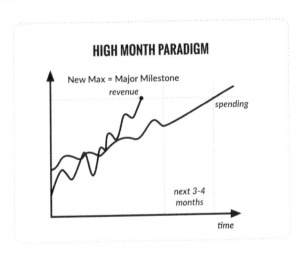

And to get a bit more specific about the way risk tends to materialize in your business, my experience has shown me that three months after their highest-revenue month, businesses tend to take on a significant amount of *new* expenses, putting them in a worse position and carrying more risk.

This is because as revenues go up, a business typically

makes assumptions about the trend line, acquires more fixed expenses and oftentimes, their cash flow goes down, taking the business owner in question farther and farther away from the goals they've set or, in this case, priorities they've identified. This situation is an excellent example of problems expanding even as revenue goes up, a version of Parkinson's law.

Impact on Effort: Parkinson's Law

Parkinson's law may have started out as a joke by Cyril Northcote Parkinson in a 1955 essay he wrote for *The Economist* (later expanded into a book), but that doesn't make it any less true or any less important for our understanding of how time and effort interact with one another.

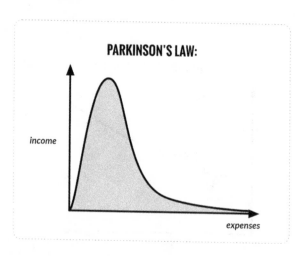

Put simply, Parkinson's law states that work expands to fill the time allotted for it. If you set aside four hours for a particular task, you will get that task done within its set four-hour slot. However, if you were to decide that you have eight hours in which to do the same task, you'll most often find that the task now takes the full eight hours to complete.

And this law also applies to your finances; without a system in place, your expenses will expand to fill the revenue amount allotted for them, too. As we make more, we spend more, which can take us farther from our set goals because we're still fixated on "more" instead of "closer" to what matters to us.

Risk Impact: Actions That Take You Further Away

There's an excellent introduction to this concept in Andy Grove's book *High Output Management*, which basically boils down to this:

You hire a new employee based on the idea that the extra manpower will save you time in the long run. But inevitably, the new reports coming from that new employee will require more management time each week—on average, four hours more.

Now you've actually cost yourself a lot of the time you were hoping to save. In the same way that more revenue does not necessarily mean more progress toward your priorities, more staff does not usually equal time saved. You've just added more risk and, in the short term, gotten farther away from what actually matters.

Optionality Impact: Readiness and Rhythm

In terms of reducing risk, readiness (as I use the term here) describes your ability to take on more of something. This could mean more clients, more staff, more revenue or what have you.

Readiness is an algorithm built into a web application I created called The Certainty App™ (CertaintyApp.com). Don't worry, I'll discuss The Certainty App™ in more detail later in the book.

What I can tell you from years of looking at the data is after their highest revenue month, most companies have a low readiness score. In other words, they are not ready to take on more until they normalize the new level they're at and get enough data for a new trend line. At a high level, the readiness score can be broken down into Industry Rhythm, Business Decision Rhythm and Personal Rhythm.

In trying to find a way through whatever problems you're facing, consider the fact that you may actually be trying to solve issues that can't be solved. More accurately, you may be trying to outspend or outsell something that can't be solved with either of those approaches or indeed with any approach that values adding *more* of anything.

Part of why this happens is that you could be in a situation where you find yourself fighting against rhythms or trends trying to gather more and more of whatever resource, when you should be trying to get closer to your priorities instead.

When I was the president of the Seattle University Alumni Board of Governors, I was fortunate to work with some former Microsoft executives. They talked with me about a common parlance within the company that they called "The Rhythm of the Business." That is, for a year or the course of a product launch, there are predictable events (rhythms) that occur. I took that concept and deconstructed it further because, while big corporations are their own entity and thus you can simplify it down to "rhythm of the business," a small business is more delicate.

You can boil this larger concept down to three types of rhythms business owners run up against:

Industry Rhythm: Any industry rhythm is the ebb and flow that comes with the territory of a specific industry. For example, in my accounting firm, the end-of-year and tax deadlines are going to be busy no matter what. In other words, there are natural peaks and valleys specific to your industry.

In the fitness industry, we often see that New Year's resolutions cause an uptick in gym memberships and health food purchases. In e-commerce, Black Friday and Cyber Monday deals lead to November and December peak revenue months.

Business Decision Rhythm: These are business decisions that we've made. They include the decisions we make about setting up our business, including billing cycles and billing structure.

A gym, for example, may have a spike in business revenue that results in a disproportionate spike in monthly revenue because they decided to collect a year of membership up front instead of monthly. In this case, the industry rhythm (New Year's resolutioners looking for a gym membership) and a business decision to charge a year up front will create a revenue spike that isn't necessarily indicative of what future months will look like.

Personal/Individual Rhythm: We have our own personal business rhythm. Remember my example in the previous section about not making decisions in January? This is a *me* thing, and it's a unique, individual rhythm.

Industry rhythms, for the most part, we can't do anything about. I can't change the tax deadline or control the new tax laws. The business decisions and individual rhythm, however, I do have control over. The way we want to change these decisions is to change them in a way that actually gets me closer to the things that I want.

Although some of these rhythms may be correlated or have some overlap as we see in the gym example above, we are often ignorant to the fact that they are separate and have different natures, which results in us spending time and energy on things we have no control over and neglecting the things we do have control over.

If we focus on "more" instead of "closer" to what we want, we run the risk of ignoring our business rhythms and getting further away from it.

Rig the Game:

- Without a destination in mind, we risk the accumulation of "more" taking us farther away from what we want.
- As profit increases, so does the risk of loss.
- When we make the effort to choose "closer" over "more," it is important to understand the different rhythms that impact our business decisions.

6

CERTAINTY COMMANDMENT #2:

PREFERENCE VERSUS BINARY

I f I asked you if I should buy a house to renovate, launch a marketing campaign for my business or work with my spouse, what would you say?

Would you know how to advise me? Would you give me a "right" or "wrong" answer? If I asked five different people, I'd most likely get five different answers, right? How would Gary respond?

I'd then be left with even more uncertainty because I didn't know the right answer. So what is the right answer? Again, it depends.

The real question is: What do I want? Or put another way: What am I trying to get closer to?

To answer this question, it requires actually knowing what I want before I ask the question in the first place.

While I've introduced the idea of preferences and the role that they play in our decision-making, it bears further exploration. Because when it comes to business or finance, a lot of people tend to adopt a right-or-wrong mentality—or a binary. And there are plenty of voices on the internet that encourage this type of thinking.

Let's start with when we're young. As we go through school, we lose our creativity. We start to conform. And we buy into narratives that you need to be a creative genius in order to succeed. In education, there are standards. If you exceed those standards, you're considered smart. As we introduced in Chapter 2, Playing Your Game, teaching smart people is actually the hardest.

There's often a gap between espoused values and values in action—and what's worse is that we now expect instantaneous answers. This dynamic feeds into the narrative that in every domain and subdomain, there is a right and a wrong. Yet we could ask 10 people questions like, "Should I buy a house? or Should I hire employees?" and get 10 different explanations for their answers. That's because we must understand that almost every question we ask is actually a preference-based question.

In other words, there's no right or wrong. It depends on what you want. When you don't understand that a question you're asking is a preference, then you create more uncertainty. You're running the risk of getting an answer that you take as fact getting you further away from what you want.

In my experience—and from years of working with clients —this is what I've observed:

We could take two business owners in the same industry who have the same revenue, size and number of partners and they could still want totally different things. One business owner could want to grow their business to double where it is right now. The other might say, "I don't care about growing my business anymore. I just want more time."

So they're in the same exact business with the same amount of revenue, yet they want different things. *And they are both correct.* The point is that the business decisions we're facing are preference-based. That means you have to get clear on what it is that you actually want.

When I raise the idea of "what you actually want," a

common response is: well, what is a good "want"? I will provide a more detailed blueprint for this under Part 4, but there is no "good" or "bad" want (okay, you could come up with something morally or ethically bad). If there were a "good" or "bad" want, then there wouldn't be preferences. Everything would be binary. But fortunately, everything is not binary.

The next most commonly asked question is, "How do I distinguish between preference and binary?"

That's when we turn to WWGD: What Would Google Do? Can the question you're asking yourself be solved with a Google search?

In your day-to-day, questions might look something like this:

"Should I scale my business?"
"Should I hire a nanny first or an executive admin?"
"Should I buy a house or rent?"
"Should I invest in this marketing campaign?"
"Should I work with my spouse?"
"Should I hire employees or contractors?"
"Should I raise my prices?"
"Should I launch this new product?"
"Should I offshore part or all of my team?"
"Should I build a marketing funnel?"
"Should I turn this home into a rental property?"
"Should I renovate my home or sell it and buy a new home?"

And here's the nefarious answer to each of the above: it depends. These answers are not binary. Google may return millions of hits to each of those questions, but as you read through the search results, you'll find a caveat or an underlying anxiety that's stopping you from implementing the recommendations.

Inherently, you know there is not a right or wrong or universal true or false to the questions you're asking. I'd argue that's one of the joys of business and life. It's also where the dynamic complexity exists.

See, not only do the answers to questions like these vary, they depend on *your specific preferences*. You need to ask yourself: What are you prioritizing?

The correct answer for one person may be different from the correct answer for another person in the same position. In the case of the nanny versus admin question, if spending more time with your kids is a priority for you, then the admin would be the best move. If not, the reverse may get you closer to what you really want.

You simply can't get the complete, final answer from Google. If you could get all your answers from an algorithm, we wouldn't have consulting businesses. Quite simply, we wouldn't need them. But, like a lot of topics discussed in books or podcasts aimed at entrepreneurs, what sounds straightforward in theory is a lot harder to work through in real life.

This Commandment is a warning against overgeneralized black-and-white answers. When we subscribe to what we believe to be universal cookie-cutter answers to our questions, everyone gets stuck doing what they "should" do, and no one ever really gets what they want.

Impact on Effort: Lost Momentum = Opportunity Cost

By the definition found in any physics textbook, *momentum = mass x velocity*.

Newton's first law of motion teaches us that, "An object at rest stays at rest, and an object in motion stays in motion with the same speed and in the same direction unless acted upon by an unbalanced force."

It also states that: "Conservation of momentum is a fundamental law of physics which states that the momentum of a system is constant if there are no external forces acting on the system." It is embodied in Newton's first law (the law of inertia). In this case, the business owner is the force acting against the system.

And how do you lose momentum? You apply friction to it, thereby reducing acceleration. So what is the friction that exists in our business? It's *us*. We're the ones applying the friction that causes lost momentum. And we cause this friction when we try to build out elaborate spreadsheets that don't actually answer our questions. Inherently, we still know that there's a preference, but we tried to make it an algorithm with a "right or wrong" lens. And all that happens is that we look at our useless spreadsheets and we go, "Well, this doesn't really tell me anything because I made so many assumptions, so I still don't know what I should do next."

Momentum is everything in business. The term "momentum" refers to the quantity of motion that an object has. Any object with momentum is going to be hard to stop, and it's much easier to steer, pivot or direct an object with momentum behind it. One of the serious consequences of binary thinking is that it can be a complete and total momentum killer.

Perhaps the most common question I get is: Should I make this investment (hire someone, start a marketing campaign)? When you're locked into binary thinking, you believe that there is a right or wrong answer and you're in search of the tool to give you that answer. I suppose you could just use a Magic Eight Ball that tells you only "yes" or "no." In conventional finance, we would have financial forecasts and KPIs that would guide us in this decision-making process. Those are maintained by finance people for finance people to use in their decision-making. I discuss this further in the book when I talk about the principle First We Optimize, Then We Maximize.

Should you hire someone? Should you start this marketing

campaign? Well, what are your priorities? What are your current cash reserves? As we answer these questions, we can more quickly discern whether the outcome would get us closer or further from what we want. The spreadsheets have a use but they're a momentum killer if we haven't first run the questions through the filter of what we want.

Understanding our preferences allows us to strategize and execute with our preferences driving the strategy, so that we don't have to do things that do not feel aligned or that require us to stop, learn a new skill and then have to start again. Binary thinking is detrimental to your momentum because it tends to result in a lack of action, and can wind up limiting your cash flow in terms of opportunity cost.

Impact on Risk: Cognitive Burden

Cognitive burden is an unaccounted-for cost.

This isn't something that's taught in business school because there are teams that exist to handle each component of the business. For example, the accounting team creates reports that they then review and update. Same with the marketing team. When you're a small business owner, you are often the whole team or the final decision-maker. Each additional responsibility becomes a weight you have to carry around.

So when should you account for this extra cost? Here are some examples:

When you hire a marketing agency and they tell you the cost is $2,500 per month, that is not the full cost. We need to account for how much time you'll have to spend thinking about it as well as how that extra burden might take you away from other investments or activities.

There's a lot of generalized information about debt. Some, like finance expert Dave Ramsey, say to never carry any debt. Others might tell you to always use leverage and reason with a math-based argument. What's left out is the cognitive burden of having to think about the debt. For some, they will lose sleep over it and be frozen around adding new decisions. That means the cost is not, say six percent per year, but six percent plus the cost of lost sleep and the loss of any returns on decisions that they had to forego. So perhaps the actual cost is more like 12 to 16 percent. That's important to know when doing the math to determine if the return on the debt is worthwhile.

The risk as it relates to ignoring preferences versus binary thinking in relation to cognitive burden is that we get so stuck in thinking that there's a right way and a wrong way that we carry this tremendous cognitive burden and arrest all progress. That is to say, when we don't properly characterize whether something is a preference versus a binary (right or wrong) and just default to it being binary. Then we spend hours, days or weeks in a swirl trying to find the "right answer" only to not make any progress at all.

Any business owner who received a fairly traditional business education (business schools, coaches) probably spends a lot of time building elaborate spreadsheets to keep track of costs and expenses. Most of them do this simply because it's what they were taught to do. But these spreadsheets—and really, this entire way of thinking—don't typically account for cognitive burden or the amount of brain power you will need to consume to execute the strategy.

A whole host of important non-financial costs get left out when cognitive burden is glossed over, including cost to your bandwidth, the cost of being completely bogged down and the cost of running out of cognitive horsepower altogether. All these factors related to your cognitive burden will invariably affect your cash flow.

If you reduce the cost of cognitive burden, it becomes a sunk cost that can be recaptured and reallocated somewhere else or into something more profitable that gets you closer to what matters most.

Impact on Options: Missing More Efficient Solutions

When you think in binary terms, you are playing a game of right and wrong. It's obvious that narrowly considering an issue at hand can cause us to miss out on a wide swath of potential solutions—solutions that would be better suited to the specific issues we're having—and yet we do it anyway. We are calibrated and conditioned to strive for accuracy but let's expand our thinking to incorporate another nuance: completeness.

So, what is completeness? I think it's easiest explained with an example: Let's consider your bank account. Say you're trying to reconcile a bank account in a financial software like Quick-Books and you notice that the bank statement shows $100 but the software shows $99. From an accuracy standpoint, you're only off by $1. Who cares about a $1 difference? Let's pass and move on—life is too short, after all.

Before we pass and move on, completeness compels us to expand our analysis to look beyond just the balance difference and ask the question: have we captured all the transactions? That $1 difference could actually be comprised of 3,000 transactions that all offset to the $1 difference. And, when we add in all those transactions we find out that we made *a lot* more than we'd realized and also spent *a lot* more.

That extra insight you gain from seeing the full picture of how much you've made and spent could materially alter your thinking in a way that the $1 difference might not. So the pivot in moments where we recognize binary thinking is to pause and ask: Have I considered all the possible solutions?

If the answer is "no" and we are committed to an orientation that results in the least effort with the least risk and the most amount of optionality, then we are compelled to compile a complete list, to the best of our abilities, of all potential solutions.

Once we have a complete list, we can apply success probabilities to each potential outcome to determine the option with the highest probability of success (this concept is called Expected Value).

See, the risk in the binary framework, the black-and-white, yes-or-no thinking, is that we randomly come up with an answer. For example, due to the recency bias, we may believe that the way someone told us to solve a problem last week is the only way to solve it. And we get fixated on that. But that's the equivalent of blindly searching for a needle in a haystack. Maybe we get lucky and randomly land on the best solution, but probably not. We tend to fail more often than not because we don't see every possible solution. But when we see every possible solution, we are inherently biasing optionality.

Rig the Game:

- Our affinity to think in binary terms limits our ability to properly evaluate our wants.
- Taking in our specific preferences in every financial decision ensures a clearer path to what we want.
- When locked into binary thinking, we add cognitive burden and put a strain on our momentum and efficiency toward reaching our goals.

7

CERTAINTY COMMANDMENT #3:

EVERY DECISION HAS INFINITE TRADE-OFFS

There are two major takeaways from this Commandment.

First, resources are scarce. An investment of money in one initiative removes an infinite number of other possible investments. Further, a commitment of time or energy to one initiative removes an infinite number of other initiatives we could have committed the same time or energy toward.

Cognitive distortions make it difficult for most of us to fathom the concept of infinite and, as Virginia Satir established, "we tend to prefer the certainty of misery over the misery of uncertainty." So, when faced with an opportunity to invest, we might be inclined to assume, *I've got to invest now because this opportunity won't exist again.* And, in doing so, we've now tied up our capital and cannot participate in other opportunities.

Regardless of if you can conceptualize it at your current station in life, there are, in fact, an infinite number of other investment opportunities. There are an infinite number of ways you could spend your time and energy. So we must exercise restraint until we have clarity that the decision we make to allocate resources provides the highest probability of getting us closer to what we want with the least amount of effort and the least amount of risk, and leaves open the most amount of options.

Second, we need to stop allowing ourselves to be victims in our own business and life. As an example, I talk to a lot of business owners who say, "I'm a visionary, so I just need someone who can operate the business while I do my visionary stuff." If you divorce yourself from an entire portion of your business or life, you will never fully understand the consequences of your actions and will be unable to see the trade-offs that exist within them.

Let's say, for example, that you decide you only want to focus on marketing and sales and don't want to be involved in the finances (the equivalent in your personal life would be that you only want to make the money but you don't want to be responsible for spending the money and you ask your spouse to own all of that without you). What you're actually doing is setting up the person in finance (or your spouse) to be the villain, and you become the victim.

This idea that you can somehow run a business and not have to be a part of the financial side of things is unfortunately not realistic, and it's how you end up in a self-victimization loop that sounds a lot like, "I just got into business because I want to do the fun stuff! I didn't realize I had to deal with money, too." But when you make a sale, you collect money. That's the financial outcome of your action. And we get stuck in marketing. We want to do more marketing in order to make more sales, but those sales then go into our bank account. How do we then get to ignore the finances?

We don't. There's just no way to separate your business decisions from your financial ones. They are one and the same, inextricably bound together. And one of the foremost reasons we need to keep this assumption top-of-mind is that when we don't, we risk making business decisions that have financial consequences we weren't expecting. Unrealistically dividing our business decisions from the ones that drive our finances can land us with an outcome we were not prepared for.

Impact on Effort: My Time Is Too Valuable

A common way for this effect to manifest is to assume that your time is "too valuable." That assumption often projects that certain tasks are beneath you, or projects and tasks that seem simple to you are a waste of your time, energy and resources. But is your time really that valuable? Because if that assumption is wrong, you're trading money for time and thinking it's getting you closer to your goals when it's actually getting you further away. And, consequently, by working on the wrong things, you've allocated your effort incorrectly.

Here's what I see more often than not when examining small businesses: The owners and leaders have outsourced a lot of their tasks under the guise of "my time is too valuable" but really the reasoning was simply "I don't like (insert task)." Then when we look at the profitability of the business, they are barely getting by—or worse, they are losing money, month after month, year after year.

So, let's talk about how to actually evaluate the value of your time in your business. Take your profits plus your wages and divide that by how many hours you work. For example, if your profits plus wages total $100,000 and you work 2,000 hours per year, then the value of your time is $50 per hour ($100,000 / 2,000 hours). If your profits plus wages are a negative number, say -$50,000, and you work 2,000 hours, then every hour you work is -$25.

In many masterminds and throughout social media, however, you're likely to find hyperbolic advice like, "Anything less than $200/hour should be outsourced because your time is too valuable." But if you do the math and your hourly rate is something like the examples above of $50 or -$25, respectively, then you might want to reconsider the tasks you're outsourcing that cost more than your effective hourly rate.

Now you might be experiencing this visceral reaction: *Dan, are you saying I now need to take back all these tasks that I hate?*

And the answer is: it depends.

If you're losing money and outsourcing a bunch of tasks that you have the capacity and capability to handle, then you might want to consider taking those tasks back.

However, that's not really the point.

The point is to ask a better and deeper question: How can I leverage the time I've freed up so that I get a better return?

In other words, the data suggests that you are putting in too much effort because you're not working on the tasks that yield the highest leverage in your business (because if you were, you'd have a higher hourly rate).

The point is not necessarily to take on more tasks. The point is to test your assumptions about the value of your time. It might mean more tasks in the short term, but ultimately, you need to design a better system so that you get a greater return on your investments.

It can be emotionally draining to have this sudden awareness that our time, as measured by the numbers, is not as "valuable" as we once thought. So I want to recognize that for many people, this can be very triggering.

And I want to really emphasize that trade-offs are infinite and evolving. Consequently, recovering and reallocating resources is an ongoing game, not a one-time, set-it-and-forget-it endeavor. The endgame, however, is the ultimate reward: your effort is matched with the work that will get you to what you want the fastest.

Impact on Risk: Not Understanding What You're Actually Working Toward

The biggest risk is not whether we have enough money. Or enough time, for that matter.

The biggest risk is that we don't get what we want out of our life. Full stop.

That means we have to be clear on what we're actually working toward. Otherwise, the trade-offs are inherently misaligned and the consequences are potentially dire (you're getting further away from what you want).

To pick an extreme, imagine you're drowning.

What is the first thing you need to decide?

When I ask this question at speaking events, the inevitable answer is: how to stop drowning.

But if we dig a little deeper, that's not the first thing you need to decide.

The first thing we need to decide is that we want to survive. Believe it or not, there is a choice, and I'd say a declaration, that needs to be made that we want to survive. And in making that declaration, we summon the will to live and tap into the resources needed to give ourselves the best probability of getting our head above water.

However, if we wait too long, the resources required to recover may move from possible to impossible.

Too many times, however, I see people figuratively drowning. What are they doing with their time?

They are talking about self-actualizing.

These people often make statements like, "Life's too short for this. What I really want out of life is (insert proclamation about being the most they can be here)."

While those statements may be true, what's the trade-off of not having absolute clarity toward what you're working toward?

Well, in the literal sense of drowning, the time we spent

self-actualizing could have been used to get our head back above water. Instead, we sank further down and now require more resources to get our head back above water.

The same is true in the figurative sense. When we declare we are drowning (in work, life, relationships) and when we elect to first self-actualize or simply first pursue absolute clarity on what we are working toward, the trade-off is perhaps the biggest risk of all: the certainty that we're not getting what we want out of life.

Impact on Optionality: Decreased System Reliability

"When you fail to plan, you plan to fail," said most parents to their kids. This statement implies that the existence of a plan provides reliability. Reliability, as defined by Merriam-Webster, is "the extent to which an experiment, test or measuring procedure yields the same results on repeated trials." In other words, something is reliable if it produces the desired results (namely, it doesn't fail).

If you've ever tried to do something innovative, you know that there are a host of both known unknowns and unknown unknowns. It would therefore follow that any plan would have to be flexible enough to change. Perhaps the hyperbolic statement should then be, "When you fail to plan on failing, you plan to fail."

In fact, each step in a plan that doesn't have a 100 percent probability of success reduces the reliability of the overall plan. As an example, let's say we have a three-step plan.

The reliability of the plan is the product of each step's probability of success. To explain that in layman's terms, let's say that the probability of success for each step is as follows:

Step 1: 100 percent probability of success
Step 2: 80 percent probability of success
Step 3: 100 percent probability of success

So what's the probability of success for the full plan? It's 80 percent. That's arrived at by multiplying each step together: 100 percent x 80 percent x 100 percent = 80 percent.

What this demonstrates is that any step in the process that is less than 100 percent reduces the overall reliability of the plan.

To illustrate this further, if we added a fourth step with a 50 percent probability of success, the new overall reliability of the plan becomes 40 percent.

This is arrived at as follows: 100 percent x 80 percent x 100 percent x 50 percent = 40 percent.

So even if we added a fifth step with a 100 percent probability of success, the overall reliability remains at 40 percent. We could also add five more steps each with a 100 percent probability of success and, guess what, the overall plan would still be at 40 percent.

So what's the point? We think we need a plan, so we build something very detailed and that calms our anxiety (for the moment).

But if any step in the process doesn't have 100 percent probability of success, then we've necessarily created a plan that has less than 100 percent probability of going "according to plan."

In fact, each step further you get down the list inherently tends to have less than 100 percent probability of success. So each step you add further decreases the probability of success.

We've built a rigid plan that reduces our optionality because it's a plan we made—so of course we have to follow it. However, what we've really done is increase the odds of dooming ourselves to failure.

What's the alternative? Simply, we must acknowledge that

any step with less than 100 percent probability of success has to remain flexible to change. And in doing so, when we approach each step, we examine *all* possibilities (trade-offs) that we can avail ourselves of so we can choose the option with the highest probability of success.

Rig the Game:

- Decisions can't exist in a vacuum since a decision to invest a resource removes an infinite number of other options.
- We must be clear on what it is that we are actually working toward or we can't properly weigh the trade-offs.
- Designing a "fail-proof plan" might limit our options and doom us to failure. Whenever possible, leave all options open so you can evaluate all alternatives one step at a time.

8

CERTAINTY COMMANDMENT #4:

BUSINESS DECISIONS SHOULD HAVE ASYMMETRIC UPSIDE

Raise your hand if you're a gambler. Craps table not your thing? Maybe you're more of a poker player.

The simple truth is that business is basically gambling and we're essentially 100 percent commission. But we don't want to admit that because what would our friends and family think? They'd probably scrutinize us much more if they thought we had an actual gambling problem, especially when our salaries can be unpredictable.

No matter how smart or meticulous you are, if you are an entrepreneur, you are a gambler. You're going to have to make more than a few bets as you go along, and believe it or not, there are ways to assess these bets and determine whether they might be worthwhile.

The question we must stop and ask ourselves, however, is whether these bets will get us closer to what we want without taking on too much risk. You might be wondering, "Where do I draw the line?"

Without really understanding risk and trade-offs, that probably feels like an impossible question to answer.

Can you really afford to gamble the rent money? Intuitively, we know that money is not infinite. There are trade-offs. When we bet on one opportunity, it removes an infinite number of other bets we could have made. But we don't think like that. We get stuck in cognitive distortions like all-or-nothing thinking. Or overgeneralizations. Or comparing ourselves to overly successful a-holes like Gary. The consequences of this are dire.

That is why we must think in terms of asymmetry. Taking the Merriam-Webster definition, asymmetry means "having two sides or halves that are not the same: not symmetrical."

As it relates to asymmetric risk, there are two sides: asymmetry to the downside and asymmetry to the upside. When you have an asymmetry to the downside, that means that the risk of a bad outcome is greater than the risk of a good outcome. Conversely, asymmetry to the upside represents that the risk of a bad outcome is less than the risk of a good outcome. Conventionally, when this term is used in finance, people think of asymmetry in multiples—that is an asymmetric bet to the upside would mean that the upside substantially outweighs the downside.

It's a strange paradigm in entrepreneurship circles, however. Many entrepreneurs are making bets where, at best, the risk is equal to the reward and, at worst, the risk is the equivalent of scorched earth while the reward is a modest return.

It's time to break that paradigm.

As illustrated in the diagram, we want to eliminate asymmetric risk to the downside and, frankly, risk where the upside and downside are equal. That means we're only leaving asymmetry to the upside (and ideally, a substantial upside).

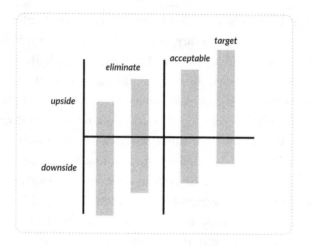

To do that, we must first remove the veil over strategy. The term strategy is a wolf in sheep's clothing. It allows us to mask what we're really doing—we are making a bet. And when you're betting, you're gambling. Now, gambling has a bad connotation in the context of business because we know, at the casino, the house wins more times than not. And, surely, we are smarter than that, right? We wouldn't want to tell our friends, family, clients and spouses that we are professional gamblers, as they might think we're crazy.

But, alas, the data says that most businesses don't survive past five years and even fewer make it past 10.

So here we are, face-to-face with the reality that what we call strategy is really a bet. Now, just because it's a bet doesn't mean we haven't done the requisite work to justify the cost, but once we acknowledge the risks, we are really taking its cause for further self-reflection.

To confuse things further, money, as any parent would be quick to comment, "doesn't grow on trees." Money is a scarce resource. It generally has to be earned, and it's not infinite. We can't simply invest in an unlimited amount of opportunities because we neither have an unlimited amount of money nor an unlimited amount of time to earn said money.

That means that if we bet money on one initiative, it will potentially restrict our ability to bet on another.

There are two main criteria for a worthy bet:

First, there's significantly more upside than downside. The best entrepreneurs out there are constantly on the lookout for asymmetric bets. Here is an expanded version of Jeff Bezos on risk:

> *Given a ten percent chance of a 100 times payoff, you should take that bet every time. But you're still going to be wrong nine times out of ten. We all know that if you swing for the fences, you're going to strike out a lot, but you're also going to hit some home runs. The difference between baseball and business, however, is that baseball has a truncated outcome distribution. When you swing, no matter how well you connect with the ball, the most runs you can get is four. In business, every once in a while, when you step up to the plate, you can score 1,000 runs.*

In other words, business owners need to be taking bets where the upside is far greater than the downside.

Second, we must *not* risk complete ruin. Another way to think about this is that we must be okay with the worst possible outcome.

Would you rather play rock-paper-scissors or Russian roulette? Both are games of chance (mostly). Only one bears the risk that you might not be able to walk away when you lose (unless you're playing a version of rock-paper-scissors that I don't know about).

Don't make bets that include the possibility of destruction to your business, your finances, your goals or your life in general. If you go all in on a game of Russian roulette, the worst outcome is that you lose your life. There are no second chances if you have a bad round. That would be the major problem with choosing to play the game.

And the other big consideration, if you're playing Russian roulette, is how repeat exposure affects your odds. Sure, you might pull the trigger once, twice, three times even and be okay afterward. But the more times you play, the higher the risk of a devastating downside becomes.

A note on repeat exposure: in a standard game of Russian roulette, at complete random, you would win five times out of six or 83.3 percent of the time. If 100 people played the game, 83% of them would likely live, but if you were to try and play the game 100 times, it's unlikely you'd survive past round six.

In less extreme terms, consider a night at the *regular* roulette tables. Each round, you place a bet. Logically, knowing the odds of the house coming out on top, you have to be aware of the risks involved when you go "all in." If you lose, you lose big. But you put your bet on the table. So you have to be okay with the worst possible outcome that may result from the decision you made.

We don't tend to think in terms of win or loss record but instead in terms of the probability of the total outcome. This is also why certain people always seem to win when others don't. The perennial winners actually lose more often. They just take more asymmetric bets with low-impact downside relative to the upside while most people take bets with far more symmetry or bets where the upside is equal to the downside.

Once we've thought through these assumptions and made a mental place for them moving forward, we can begin to take some more concrete steps to decide on the real-world things (and situations, certainties and wealth) we want to reach and fund.

While I agree with Jeff Bezos in taking 10 percent odds for a 100 times potential payoff, it's only a wise decision when 10 percent isn't going to knock you out of the game entirely.

Now, as I've already established above, the biggest risk of all is the risk that we don't get what we want out of our life. To deconstruct that further, we must acknowledge that what we want isn't necessarily just money. There are other "currencies" to consider, which include but are not limited to: time, influence, energy and reputation.

Therefore, when we are evaluating for asymmetry, we need to be rooted in what currency or currencies we are optimizing toward. If, for example, our primary currency is energy and we take on a client that produces a lot of money with little to no financial downsides but sucks all of our energy, we entered into an arrangement that was asymmetrical to the downside.

Impact on Effort: Guaranteeing You Have to Work Until "Retirement Age"

The most common answer I receive when I ask someone why they wanted to start a business is: freedom. When I drill down on that further, it's usually expanded to, "I want to have the option to work with whom I want, when I want."

That totally resonates with me.

For most, "working on your terms" is not much different from being able to retire. That is, you're able to work on your terms because you don't actually need to work to maintain your lifestyle.

Sadly, most have designed a system that guarantees they will have to work until retirement age.

It's simple but hard to accept.

When all your bets have more downside than upside, you've constructed a system with chaos built in.

You may have periods where cash flow is strong. However, when you take that excess cash and invest in more bets that have an asymmetry to the downside, you've doomed yourself to needing more effort to recover.

More times than I can count, I've talked to a business owner and they tell me how they are crushing it with all these great new initiatives that will remove them from the business. Then, three months later, we talk and they are nearly out of cash and scrambling. All momentum is lost so they have to expend a metric ton of effort just to get back to breakeven.

Changing your orientation toward making asymmetric bets to the upside doesn't guarantee that you won't go through that same cash flow roller coaster. It does, however, put you in a much better position to avoid ruin while also having bets that could push you into retirement status seemingly overnight.

Impact on Risk: We Just Can't See It

Most of us just aren't wired to naturally see asymmetry to the upside. No judgment. I would include myself in that statement, and I don't feel any shame about it.

Most of us, however, don't want to think that we are most of us.

Those who naturally see it or manufacture it (for example, Elon Musk) are an infinitesimal portion of the population. And that's okay. The rest of us just need to acknowledge that it's a blind spot and be intentional about finding asymmetry to the upside.

The risk is that we won't. And we won't because we're blinded by our biases.

It's easier to rationalize a decision through all-or-nothing thinking, loss aversion, anchoring bias and so on. And while we do it, we'll be shouting from the rooftops that we're making an entirely rationalized decision and everyone should support our decision-making.

So it's obvious that the impact on the risk of violating this commandment is more risk. However, it needs to be called out and repeated ad nauseam in hopes that in doing so, you'll create enough space between each decision to try to work through your biases and give yourself a fighting chance to make an asymmetrical decision to the upside.

Impact to Optionality: Survival Mode

When you take on too much risk and the bets don't pay off, you burn through resources. When you have limited resources, you have limited options.

You put yourself in survival mode.

Now this is when someone will argue that they are best when their back is up against the wall. And if that is true, then I'd suggest WWMJD: What Would Michael Jordan Do?

If you watched the documentary *The Last Dance*, you saw stories of Michael Jordan manufacturing enemies so he would have someone to rise against in a game. It might be the way someone looked at him or something they uttered, when in actuality they weren't necessarily enemies. The takeaway is that you don't have to actually wreck yourself to create scenarios that bring out the best in yourself.

So if you know that you're at your best with limited options, then manufacture that scenario for yourself without the actual ruin. For example, if you find you operate better when there's less money in your business bank account, transfer the funds somewhere that you can't see the balance and it's difficult to access the funds.

This concept is hedging the downside. That is, we are actively using tools and tactics to eliminate the bad stuff. And if you eliminate all the bad stuff, then you're only left with either things you're okay with or things that are good.

So rather than intentionally back yourself into a corner where you're out of options operating in survival mode, think about how you can create the motivations you need to get the outcome you want without the associated risk.

Rig the Game:

- Business is always going to be a gamble, but when you approach the risks asymmetrically, you'll have a more accurate view of the possible outcomes.
- There is no strategy to employ when making a bet on your business, but the upside generally outweighs the downside in asymmetrical thinking.
- The financial risks of gambling with your business decisions are always present; mitigating the risk comes from knowing your limits and anticipating the worst.

"The greatest test of your expertise is how explicitly you understand your assumptions."
—*Kevin Ashton*

PART III

OPERATING SYSTEM ALGORITHMS

9

USING BETTER ALGORITHMS

One of the hallmarks of how most entrepreneurs (including me) operate is that we like to live in states of strategy and execution. We come up with no shortage of ideas we want to implement. We research and we brainstorm or we just start doing stuff.

Additionally, we are bombarded by the internet with things we "should" be doing or "should" be focused on. By now, we understand the Certainty Commandments:

That our business exists to get us closer to what we want; that we must understand the difference between questions where the answer is "it depends" and questions that can be answered by Google; that every business decision is a financial decision; and that we will only make bets where the upside is asymmetrical.

It's through the consistent application of these Commandments that enable us to better play our game and become increasingly aware of our biases.

But in support of these Commandments, we also need the tools (or what I'm calling "algorithms" to be consistent with the operating system construct) that allow us to apply the

Commandments in a practical setting. As we established in Chapter 4, winners who consistently win carry a toolbox. And generally, it's a toolbox they've adapted to their unique disposition and priorities. Further, this toolbox must support our Commandments.

To that end, the next three chapters will walk you through the toolbox I've developed. These tools are bucketed into three categories: Frames, Issue Processors and Growth Principles.

Within each of the three categories, you'll find four tools:

1. **The Frames:** tools to provide different perspectives to navigate specifically if we are getting closer to what we want while faced with preference-based decisions.

- Parenting Frame
- Commissioner Frame
- Professional Skeptic Frame
- Investor Frame

2. **Issue Processors:** tools to evaluate possible trade-offs and allow us to find asymmetry to the upside.

- The Four Lenses
- Never Water the Weeds
- Optimize, Then Maximize
- T-Learning Over I-Learning

3. **Growth Principles:** tools that address closer versus more, aid in evaluating preference-based decisions, exploring trade-offs and finding asymmetry to the upside.

- Rely on a Preponderance of Data
- Bias Microsteps
- Consider the Rule of Three and 10
- Only Scale at the Optimal Ratios

Before you dive into these tools, there are two very important caveats.

First, as you can see in the diagram below, do not apply these tools until you've first applied the preference filter. When you apply the preference filter, you ask yourself: Will this solution get me closer to my priorities?

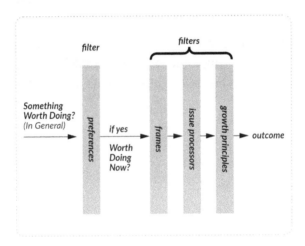

If the answer is "yes," we will now use the filters to evaluate whether the solution is worth doing now. It's important to double down on the word "now." Again, money and time are scarce resources. We may conclude a solution will get us closer to our priorities, but when weighed against other solutions with greater asymmetry, we find that doing it now is no longer the right path to funding our priorities the fastest.

Second, these are my tools. I developed them over many years. They have served me well.

Is this an exhaustive and finite list? No. Nor did I set out to have 12.

This list has been repeatedly refined. What's most important is that I have tools that are used for a specific purpose. So what I hope you take from this section is that my suggested tools are a starting point.

Make these tools your own. And as you run into issues along your path to financial certainty, do a personal archaeology dig.

Rig the Game:

1. Did I misapply the tools to the specific opportunity?
2. Did I skip using some or all of the tools?
3. What refinements do I need to make given what I know now?

10

THE FRAMES

The "frames" are like different glasses to put on when processing issues or making decisions, each one giving us a distinct perspective about what we're seeing. Applying these frames acts like a forcing function to snap you out of cognitive distortions like all-or-nothing thinking or overgeneralizations.

Back in Chapter 1, we talked about biases and I shared Dr. Jeff Spencer's framework of the Human Mindset (analogous to System 1) and the Champion's Mind (analogous to System 2). The Human Mindset gets first dibs, but if we give it a chance, the Champion's Mind has the final say. Utilizing these frames intentionally can create the space necessary to allow you to choose the Champion's Mind.

Will we always make the "right" decisions? No. But, these frames are specifically intended to put ourselves in the best position possible to get closer to what we want while navigating preference-based decisions.

Each frame has a simple question we can ask to get us into that particular frame quickly.

There are four frames:

1. **Parenting Frame:** How can I prevent something bad from happening?
2. **Commissioner Frame:** Would I be willing to play by these rules in perpetuity?
3. **Investor Frame:** Given what I know now, would I choose to opt into this particular situation?
4. **Professional Skeptic Frame:** Why? Can you prove it?

The Parenting Frame

The Parenting Frame asks: "If this were my child, how would I prevent something bad from happening?"

Starting with the Parenting Frame, let's do a small thought exercise together.

Your kids have been unusually quiet for the last few hours. As any parent knows, that's usually the first sign of trouble. When you get up to their room, they've managed to get onto, let's say, a *mature* website through that iPad you bought them for Christmas.

Like I said, trouble.

Now you've got a choice. Who do you get mad at? You could blame your kids, your TV provider or even your kids' friends.

Under the Parenting Frame, we step back and ask ourselves if we have put the systems in place to keep bad things from happening before we start to place blame on factors outside of our control.

For this, we need to introduce preventative versus detective controls.

In the accounting world, we have a tool related to this concept called internal controls. Internal controls are a mix of procedures, policies and systems to eliminate fraud and ensure the financial statements are free from material misstatements (your books are good).

When you think about trying to implement controls, there are three types: *detective, preventative* and *corrective.*

To have a complete internal control structure, we would have a mix of all three types. Preventative is the highest priority. A preventative control is exactly what it sounds like—a control preventing bad things from happening. An example of a preventative control would be requiring a signature from the owner on all checks cut to prevent the bookkeeper from misappropriating funds. Another example would be requiring a drug screen as a condition of employment.

It's rare to find a small business that has built out preventative controls. At best, they have some detective controls, meaning they find out something bad has happened and they can choose to take corrective action.

At the small business level, I find the lead domino issue tends to be that the business is built on trust. We hire someone and then trust they'll do what's right because we trust our gut (even though the data says that we're really bad at judging people's character).

I spoke with one potential client who relied entirely on one bookkeeper to handle his three companies. When I reviewed the books, they were some of the worst I'd ever seen (and I've seen thousands of books). There were three companies all combined into one QuickBooks file. That's problematic for many reasons. Namely, any attorney would tell you that when you commingle your assets, you pierce the corporate veil. That means, if one business is sued and receives a judgment against them, they could pursue assets from all the businesses and potentially personal assets as well. It's also problematic because, at best, the value of the businesses is impaired and at worst, the businesses are unsellable. A potential acquirer is going to want to review the books from inception.

When I shared my findings with the client, their response was, "Yeah, but I trust my bookkeeper." When I talked to the bookkeeper, they practically shouted me down with their resumé and accolades. Now, at this point, I didn't have the data to know if they were simply incompetent, ignorant or stealing. This is why we need to bias having preventative controls. With preventative controls in place, we can find a solution more efficiently because we can remove fraud from the equation. And ultimately, the consequence of running your business off trust is that at some point, an error occurs that could have been prevented and an otherwise good relationship is now destroyed.

This is why we want to utilize the parenting frame when analyzing opportunities and solutions.

We start with:

What is the worst that can happen? And would I be okay if that worst-case scenario occurred?

Then we examine the worst-to-best case scenarios and ask the questions:

How can we prevent bad scenarios from happening?

How can we eliminate all downside risks?

Consistent application of the parenting frame allows you to hone the skill of identifying and creating asymmetric risk to the upside. You become more adept at identifying if something is inherently asymmetric to the upside because you'll be able to more quickly see all the downsides that you can measure against the upsides. Often, we just get blinded by best-case scenarios. You'll also become more adept at creating asymmetric risks to the upside because you'll hone your abilities to eliminate the downside risks. We'll cover more of how to hedge the downside under the Four Lenses.

Going back to our mature website example, if we want the upside of having independent children who don't need round-the-clock supervision, we have to mitigate the downside risk by setting up parental controls on the devices they can access. This would be an example of preventive controls. For my own daughters, I've set Netflix to make sure they can't watch R-rated movies. I am taking steps to prevent them from seeing something that I prefer they don't see at their age.

But in terms of your business decisions, implementing preventive controls means turning a risky (or just bad) bet into a good one by setting up systems to make sure the worst-case scenario that might result from the decision you made isn't truly all that bad.

The other approach under the Parenting Frame is detective controls. Say I get an email out of the blue one day from Netflix, giving me a list of recent content my kids have been watching, and based on the report, it looks like *Die Hard* is their favorite Christmas movie, but I really wish they hadn't watched it because they're still little and not quite ready for that kind of content. Detective controls come into play when we find out something bad has happened after the fact. That's not favorable. We want a preventive over the detective.

As an aside, a basic example of a preventive control is setting a spending limit on your debit card. The limit will prevent you from spending in excess. A detective control would be receiving an alert after the transaction is complete that you've exceeded your daily spending. If our ultimate goal is to limit our spending, the preventive control is going to give us the highest level of safety.

There's one more facet to the Parenting Frame besides preventing bad things from happening or reacting to them when they do, and that is *celebrating* when things don't go wrong.

That's not an intuitive state of mind for most of humanity. Frankly, although we may not always realize it, we love when things go sideways because we love to celebrate a recovery. Think about it this way:

Your best friend decides to go on a life-changing diet, and lo and behold, they manage to drop 60 pounds! So we go all in for that person. We leave encouraging comments on the Facebook status with their before-and-after picture set, we cheer them on and we hold them up as an incredible success story.

Now, don't get me wrong. There's nothing inherently bad about losing weight. But you know what we don't do? We don't just walk up to our other friend who has maintained a healthy weight since their 20s and say something like, "Hey! Congrats to not gaining 60 pounds in the first place!"

And it's for good reason that we don't do things like that. Our friends would probably forego thanking us and recommend rigorous psychiatric treatment instead. But you see what I'm getting at. We would conserve so much energy and time if we could focus on putting systems in place to prevent bad things from happening instead of having to scramble to fix them once they have.

It's that kind of thinking that catapults us out of a victim mentality and into a mentality where we get to proactively choose what happens to us.

The Commissioner Frame

The Commissioner Frame looks at our business as if it's a team we own (in a league we also own) and asks: "Does this align with what I want in business? Would I be willing to play by these rules in perpetuity?"

To explain the Commissioner Frame, I want you to think about the commissioner of a sports league. This is the person who sets all the rules and principles by which the game is played, and therefore, the spirit of the game itself. That's the really vital piece—the spirit of the game or its intention.

I'd venture a guess that a lot of us aren't huge fans of playing games with too many rules. If we have to spend the majority of our time tending to regulation after regulation, we're probably not having much fun. We lose the enjoyment that comes with participating, competing or even winning. But some rules are necessary and, in our businesses, we are the commissioner who gets to determine what those rules are. How do we set parameters that keep the spirit of the game alive and enjoyable?

The fact is, we do tend to forget to look at business as a game (and it is). We need rules and we need principles, which are two different structures, by the way. Rules are the hard-and-fast boundaries you don't cross, and principles are more akin to guidelines. Put another way, if rules are a stop sign, principles are the lane markers you stay between as you drive.

And it can be easy to overcorrect one way or the other, to put in too many rules for yourself and your business and find yourself feeling drained and stressed, or to lay off the rules and suffer losses of productivity, morale and relationships.

Even the NFL deals with this type of balancing act. Maybe you'll remember when it banned celebrations by players for things like touchdowns. Well, that's not much fun, so the league threw that rule out to preserve some of the inherent joy in the sport. It's all about balance. Though it seems counterintuitive, having some structure in your business, or rules of the game, allows you to compete and operate in ways that you enjoy.

The Investor Frame

The Investor Frame asks: "Given what I know now, would I choose to opt into this particular situation?"

Most people have stayed in a bad relationship for too long, and after the fact, they would tell you that if they knew beforehand what they know now, they would never have opted into that relationship in the first place. They choose to stay in it because it's familiar and easy. But by staying in this relationship, by not opting out, they're violating their own principles. It's the same as opting *into* a bad relationship. As long as we are not opting *out* of the things that we would not opt *into*, we are in violation of our own personal and economic principles.

At its most simplistic, the Investor Frame forces you to step back and ask yourself: "If I had the money required to take this action, would I?"

For example:

"The business is worth one million dollars. If I had a million dollars on hand right now, would I buy it?"

Or:

"This employee costs $100,000 per year. If I had $100,000 in cash, would I still make this hire?"

And this frame still applies even if you've already made a decision. Thinking about it in terms of stocks and bonds, just because you own those things does not mean you have to continue to own them. In fact, the best investors around have stop losses in place to help them step quickly away from a bad decision. And once they do, they find a better place to put those funds to use.

Another example where the Investor Frame is particularly helpful is what I call "convenience real estate." Say you want to be a real estate investor. You already own a house and you move in with your new spouse and decide to buy a new house. You wanted to be a real estate investor so why not just turn the property you are moving out of into a rental? It would be convenient after all!

The Investor Frame would say, "If I didn't already own this property but had the cash, would I buy this property? Is the location good? What do I expect to happen to the neighborhood?

Zooming back out to the everyday entrepreneur, that kind of comfort level with loss is a completely foreign concept. Most people are extremely loss-averse by nature and will do just about anything to keep away from a bad investment.

There's also the attachment side of human nature to consider when we look at problems that might be mitigated by the Investor Frame. I like to call this tendency Naming the Puppy.

If you're an animal lover, you may know where I'm going with this. You're at a dog shelter with your friend, just looking, maybe sort of considering getting a pet, but by no means are you ready to adopt one.

Then the shelter volunteer asks if you'd like to hold the beagle puppy in the crate across the aisle. Of course, you say yes (as if there were another option). Now you've got an armful of a warm, snuggly, soulful-eyed puppy and it pops into your head that he looks like his name should be George.

Now you've got a puppy.

This is a common tendency that follows a lot of business owners around. We happen to see an opportunity or have an idea that sounds kind of exciting. Some part of us gets the slightest bit attached and now we're involved. We've named the puppy.

That's another scenario that the Investor Frame can help counteract simply by helping us take a step back, look at the situation with our money, not our emotions, and reevaluate whether adopting that puppy actually makes sense in the long run.

For businesses you're actively involved in operating day-to-day, I recommend applying the Investor Frame at least quarterly. You would apply it more frequently when evaluating a friction point in your business:

Would I hire this employee again based on what is happening currently?

Would I invest in this marketing campaign again based on the current ROI?

For businesses that you're not involved in on a day-to-day basis or other passive investments, the Investor Frame is the default frame for which I view all aspects.

Now, having laid these frames out together, we need to get in the habit of cycling through them with every decision in order to keep a comprehensive view of our options and avoid slipping too far into our own biases.

The Professional Skeptic

The Professional Skeptic Frame asks: "Why? Can you prove it?"

One of the more common approaches to business (that I've witnessed, at least) is the tendency to question *everything*. People who constantly ask "Why?" fit nicely into the Professional Skeptic Frame. This is often like:

"We had a spike in sales last month...why? Was it because I did that podcast interview around that time or is it a seasonal thing? Do we have more leads around this time of year? If so, how many *more* leads do we have relative to the effort we put into generating those leads?"

Think about this one like the Socratic Method. The question is the point—a guide through a logical path—and those who bias this method of analyzing things within their business make it their mission to tunnel past the surface layer into a deeper understanding of the underlying mechanics of the thing in question. You interrogate yourself, the data, ideas or assumptions with continuous questions.

The outcome we're in search of is truth, but more importantly, we're trying to free ourselves of biases. To a degree, it's a stoic approach to counterbalance our epicurean tendencies. Epicureanism is an ancient philosophy that the Daily Stoic describes as "focused on the pursuit of pleasure, within the bounds of moderation, and the avoidance of pain."

One profession that requires a particular amount of "professional skepticism" is that of the financial auditor. These are the people who go into companies and audit their books to make sure they are "free from material misstatements" (in layman's terms: the books are good). They do this so that investors, banks and other stakeholders can rely on their books for decision-making. I've done this work before and let's just say I'm glad I don't anymore.

That said, what *is* professional skepticism?

Rather than quote auditing standards and immediately make you dread reading this far, I'll put it in my own words. Professional skepticism is a state of mind where we suspend all judgment and expectations and question the information until we have gathered sufficient evidence to determine the proper outcome. It's almost like being a three-year-old and continually asking your parents, "But why?" We are in pursuit of complete understanding.

Professional skepticism is not about being negative. It's not about being annoying. It's not about being a Debbie Downer or Negative Nelly. Now, if you put on the professional skeptic hat and you engage with a partner, employee or friend and you don't tell them what you're doing and you're not respectful with your questioning, then odds are they'll label you as negative, annoying or disrespectful.

Rig the Game:

- **Parenting Frame:** How can I prevent something bad from happening?
- **Commissioner Frame:** Would I be willing to play by these rules in perpetuity?
- **Investor Frame:** Given what I know now, would I choose to opt into this particular situation?
- **Professional Skeptic Frame:** Why? Can you prove it?

11

THE ISSUE PROCESSORS

Now that we've talked through the frames that root us in our thinking of "closer" over "more" and help us navigate through preference-based decisions, let's get into the tools that help us address the other two Commandments.

Each issue processor is specifically intended to help you determine all possible trade-offs while finding and creating asymmetry to the upside.

These issue processors are as follows:

1. **The Four Lenses:** A tool specifically designed to manufacture asymmetry.
2. **Never Water the Weeds:** A tool specifically designed to consider the trade-offs.
3. **Optimize, Then Maximize:** A tool specifically designed to eliminate the roadblocks that inherently creep up when evaluating trade-offs.
4. **T-Learning Over I-Learning:** A tool specifically designed to evaluate trade-offs and asymmetry to the upside.

The Four Lenses

A few years ago, Nic, a business partner of mine, had four or five different courses that he wanted to launch, and he wasn't sure which one would be best to pull the trigger on. We felt that there was demand for all of them, but instead of picking randomly, or trying to do it all, he and I went through an exercise to determine the most efficient path forward. After all, we know that resources are scarce and a choice to launch one course removes our ability to not only launch the others but work on any other project.

This is an exercise I like to call the Four Lenses, which is designed to help you create asymmetric risk as you make decisions. Essentially, the process involves looking at all the ideas or choices you're considering at the moment and determining which is going to be the highest-leverage item to implement.

It's called the Four Lenses because we are evaluating the opportunity through four different "lenses" or categories: time savings, forcing function, cost savings/reduction and revenue-producing. Under each lens, we are required to assign a value that's based on a preponderance of data (see Growth Principles). If we have no data, then we have to leave that lens as a zero. And the Professional Skeptic Frame is going to say: yeah, but can you prove it?

1. Time Savings

Let's say you've got a seven-year-old who is just now learning how to load the dishwasher, and she hasn't quite gotten the hang of it. She keeps putting dirty dishes into the washer just seconds after you've finished running it, and she's even tried to put away dishes that haven't been washed yet.

Now, you have explained the process to her about 1.3 million times in the last month, but it hasn't quite managed to stick. You're barreling toward salmonella for the whole family. What can you do?

A great way to save yourself the continual time, effort and frustration of re-explaining things would be to go get a piece of paper, write "Clean" on one side and "Dirty" on the other, superglue a magnet to a chip clip and stick that sucker to the front of the dishwasher, perhaps alongside a set of instructions that tells her when to flip the sign so there's no more confusion.

That's the idea behind time savings.

Just about every business owner knows what it's like to have to explain a key concept or method over and over again to clients or employees or a webinar audience. Utilizing time savings means finding a way to lay out the confusing information in a permanent manner that answers most (if not all) of the constant questions you receive so that you can conserve your time for new questions that pop up.

2. Forcing Function

Following the dishwasher example, making sure that the "Clean/Dirty" sign is hung on the dishwasher door forces your little one to see the information she needs before she can make her next move in loading or unloading. Not only have you saved yourself valuable time, but you've also put a measure in place to force her to consciously confront the necessary pieces she needs to complete her task correctly to cut down on errors and a further waste of resources or energy.

Forcing function can also mean forcing you to do something you planned on doing anyways. For example, say you planned on writing a book on dishwashing secrets, but someone asked you to teach a course on the topic. By committing to the course, you'd be forced to create all the content needed for the book.

When forcing function, we want to assign a value related to

the net benefit to you by completing this task that you intended to complete in the first place.

3. Cost Savings/Reduction

This falls under the umbrella of making sure we're thinking about optimization (which we'll get into more later). Does the thing you're considering represent a cost savings to you and/or your business?

It's tempting to overspend in the name of quality when we think about building something new or investing. That said, favoring things that come with a cost savings to you ensures that you keep more of your existing resources in your pocket while minimizing the risk that *just maybe* the thing you think is going to sell like hotcakes underperforms and leaves you with very little return on a sizable investment.

As an example of cost savings, some businesses I've launched in the past were with vendors who I was already paying an ongoing fee. By agreeing to launch these businesses and either partner with someone else or pay a referral fee, the existing ongoing fees were eliminated. Finding cost savings will be the hardest lens to check. Remember, our tendency is to focus on more and this compels us to focus on closer.

4. Revenue Generator

This would be the most obvious consideration for most entre-preneurs and business owners. However, remember, the requirement for each lens is that we require a preponderance of data. We don't get to plug a number in based on what we feel might happen. So while this might be the easiest on the surface to populate, it's generally the most difficult when we exercise restraint and require actual data to support our belief.

Now, in Nic's case, we were able to identify that only one of the courses checked off three of the four boxes, with the potential to check off the fourth as well. This is important because even though it generated revenue, had it not, it still would have saved cost and time and been a forcing function. Basically, even if it hadn't generated revenue, it still would have been a win:

- The course in question represented a time savings because it would ultimately save him hundreds of hours of having the same conversation over and over again.
- There was a cost savings involved because the course also served as training for staff.
- Finally, the course we decided on was a forcing function to codify and build the systems for delivery.

So there was little likelihood that it could be a loss because we made sure that the asymmetry was to the upside and there was no downside.

If an avenue forward means you stand to save costs, disseminate valuable and permanent information or resources, bring conscious attention to something vital to prevent mistakes or miscommunication *and* make you money, that's likely a high-leverage path for you to take.

Most business owners get stuck in a marketing frame, which is focused on marketing and sales. And so the question they ask themselves is, "Will this generate revenue?" But as I've explained before, we're always taking a gamble. And there's always some possibility, or probability, that it will not generate revenue.

And so here's how we rig the game in order to win no matter what: For myself or my companies to take on something new, it has to unequivocally check three of the four boxes, which means that even if it's not a revenue generator, it's a time savings, a cost savings and a forcing function. In other words, even if it doesn't generate revenue, it is a huge win in other ways. So this is the only way we do things. This is a form of symmetry and the upside is greater than the downside because even if it doesn't generate revenue, it still has other benefits to the business.

Now to take it one step further, I recommend creating a spreadsheet where you track all of your ideas and populate each of the Four Lenses with a value. Then you can sum up the value of each lens and compare it to your other ideas. If you've truly held yourself to the rigor of having a preponderance of data, the idea with the highest value would represent the thing you would do now.

Never Water the Weeds

Going along with the idea of moving ourselves nearer to the things we've decided we want, the concept of not watering the weeds is just a way of thinking about pouring resources, energy and time into items that are going to get us closer to our priorities. It's an acknowledgment that resources are scarce, and thus, we need to consider trade-offs and then allocate to opportunities with the highest upside.

Imagine you're trying to grow a beautiful garden. You add in an irrigation system and plant some seeds. You just skip one step. The garden area is overgrown with weeds and you leave them there. What happens? Do we end up with the beautiful garden we imagined?

Of course not.

What happened is that we watered the weeds. Some of the seedlings may have sprouted, but the weeds have overtaken the garden.

The actions we took, or lack of actions for that matter, got us further away from what we really wanted and depleted scarce resources along the way by investing in an activity with obvious asymmetry to the downside.

In business, we do the same thing:

→ We have non-A clients who are disruptive and create constant fire drills.

→ We have toxic employees who make demands, upset clients and expect to be well-compensated.

→ We offer a service that we resent fulfilling because the margins aren't great.

Those are the weeds in our business. And like the weeds in our garden, when watered, they will quickly overrun the seedlings. That's what weeds do.

But what do *we* usually do?

We keep the troublesome clients because we want the revenue and instead try to hire someone to work with the clients we don't like. Or we try to develop new systems and processes (hello, automation), rationalizing that it's not the client, it's our operations. Maybe we go even further and say, "I'm a visionary and need an integrator. That's why we have client issues." I see the visionary/integrator argument almost daily on social media.

As for the toxic employees, we avoid them at best or placate them at worst. If we let them go, then we might have to step in and do the work they were doing, or else train someone new to do their job—and that's time we don't want to spend. So we let that toxic employee stay around until there's a breaking point where other employees start leaving or we lose enough clients we can no longer afford them.

Then there's that service we resent fulfilling due to the margins. We feel such a strong sense of loss aversion that we continue to sell it when the opportunity presents itself. We don't raise prices. We don't tweak the service offering to improve the margin.

In each of these examples, we've watered the weeds. And in doing so, we've tied up precious resources that could have been redeployed on an infinite number of other things while also accepting a lot of downside risks.

See, the concept of "closer" over "more" is a bit abstract. We can ask ourselves, "Is this getting us closer to what we want?" and answer it sincerely but incorrectly *because* of the abstract nature of the concept.

The idea of not watering the weeds is more concrete. We can visualize it in our mind's eye. It's also more palatable to raise as an objection if you adopt it among your partners and stakeholders.

That is, someone presents a solution to an opportunity and you can interject with, "I'm worried we might be watering the weeds here."

The intention is to bring everyone back to thinking about how we should be allocating resources and considering all the trade-offs.

In every business I partner in, I install this as part of our common language. Anyone is allowed to ask me if I'm watering the weeds and vice versa. Practically speaking though, this framework is used whenever evaluating solutions to a given opportunity. After all the solutions have been presented, part of the dialogue is whether any of the options will water the weeds. In a mature organization, this will become part of your daily conversations and a portion of any manager or executive meeting will be dedicated to answering that question. Further, just like spring cleaning, ask the question quarterly, "What are the weeds in our business?" Systematically, you work through each business unit: Any weeds in operations? Any weeds within our client group? Any weeds in marketing? These weeds then filter into your quarterly and annual action plans.

Optimize, Then Maximize

Maximization, in my opinion, is the biggest trap that entrepreneurs fall into. Maximization is about defaulting to "more." Maximizing means having the most of everything: the most employees, most clients, the most amount of revenue.

To make things more complicated, the strategies you learn in business school, whether they be about marketing, accounting, operations or finance, are all about *maximizing*. It makes sense. Business school largely prepares you to work for a publicly traded company.

As the CEO of a publicly traded company (or even a company that's raised capital), you have a fiduciary responsibility to "maximize shareholder value." You must default to "more." That is in direct conflict with the idea that every action you take in business and wealth creation is intended to get you "closer" to what you want.

Pragmatically, it would be impossible to align the actions of business with the priorities of hundreds to millions of shareholders. So, alas, the business must default to "more."

As purpose-driven entrepreneurs, however, we have made different choices. We aren't answering to legions of shareholders, but rather we must answer to ourselves.

As Charlie Munger said, "Invert, always invert." When the answer isn't readily apparent, we must invert. Invert means, in so many words, doing the opposite.

So what is the opposite of maximizing? It's optimizing. Optimizing is simply asking: What is the most efficient path forward to achieve my objective? It's not about having the most of everything. In other words, optimizing is the embodiment of taking actions that get us closer to what we want. Shifting from a maximize frame to an optimize frame is effectively a hedge against defaulting to "more."

Embarrassingly, it took me many years to realize this

paradigm shift. When I started Nth Degree CPAs, part of my offering was to bring my Fortune 500 expertise to the underserved small business community. With that, I would have many conversations with business owners about how to improve their financial performance, and I'd make suggestions about implementing budgets, financial forecasts and KPIs. On occasion, I'd have a sales call and the prospect would say, "I know I need to be better with my money. I know I need to start using a budget."

We would then build those solutions for clients, and guess what would happen? The adoption rate was effectively zero. The tools were maybe looked at once and then never again.

As a people pleaser (though I have since reformed), my default assumption was always, "What am I doing wrong?" That's when I realized it. These tools have value, but who is the typical end user of these types of tools? Internal finance and accounting people. See, the Fortune 500 companies have massive teams to create these metrics and monitor them. The reports are largely created by accounting and finance people for accounting and finance people.

The purpose-driven entrepreneur needs a different set of tools that are more aligned with optimizing. They need tools to evaluate risk. That's why I developed CertaintyApp.com to allow the purpose-driven entrepreneur to define their unique wealth algorithm (a representation of what they are trying to get closer to and the progress they are making to that end), the growth and decision algorithms, dynamic bank accounts (described later and also available in the CertaintyApp™) and a process I call Cash Flow Engineering, where quarterly, we systematically identify our biases and factor in things like cognitive burden that traditional finance would not consider.

Now, paradoxically, what happens after we flip from a maximize to an optimize framework within a purpose-driven business is that we create more momentum and over the long term end up with more.

Out of the concepts introduced in this section, this is probably the one I talk about the most because this is the concept that unlocked everything for me when it clicked. I realized that all those Fortune 500 companies are laser-focused on maximizing *shareholder* value. That is the job of a Fortune 500 CEO. It is their fiduciary responsibility to make sure the company always has "more."

This is mostly because the resources of one of these big companies, while not infinite, are enough to support greater materiality—meaning they can take a million-dollar loss and not go under from it. They can make bigger bets and they have more staff and resources to go toward attacking a specific problem.

The story looks differently for a small business. Resources are limited and every decision comes with a trade-off; if we do Thing A, we won't be able to afford Thing B. So we have to optimize for the most efficient path forward, with "forward" here meaning toward those priorities we set at the start of this methodology.

More often than not, when I encounter a client, friend or connection who is stuck and deciding between two courses of action, it's because they're trying to maximize. They're trying to have it all because they want to buy the house and the car and go on the vacation, too.

But that's way too many variables and trade-offs to choose between. We need to narrow it down and figure out the main thing we're optimizing for.

One of the biggest stumbling blocks we encounter when we maximize in order to create a world where we can "have it all" is that we risk missing the fact that some of our goals (the things we should be prioritizing and optimizing to achieve) may actually be diametrically opposed to each other. If we don't follow the rule and choose to pursue every course of action at once in the name of having everything we want, we fail to eliminate the risk of entering a world where we have *none* of what we want.

T-Learning Over I-Learning

Traditional education is very I-learning specific. You get a degree in engineering and you focus specifically on that domain in every class. It is justifiable when you're in pursuit of mastery in the specific domain but it has consequences. Too much domain dependency stifles your creativity and ability to innovate. That's where T-learning comes in. As the diagram below illustrates, I-learning represents domain-dependent. It's an "I" because it represents drilling down on a specific domain. T-learning, however, represents an alternate approach—it represents that we can go across multiple disciplines and then drill down.

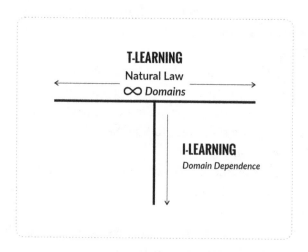

T-learning becomes the ultimate shortcut. If we're purely domain-dependent (if we work in accounting, we only look at what others in the accounting industry are doing), we are severely limited. We are looking at what's already happened in our industry or domain of choice and that is inherently limiting our creativity.

T-learning is the opposite. There are no limits to the domain we can choose. We can pull from infinite domains including natural law. See, I believe that most problems have already been solved—just maybe not in the domain you're currently working in. Thus, if we look externally, we can find the solution and then adjust it to fit the nuances of your industry or specific problem.

It's also important to distinguish that when I say problem, it can also be an opportunity. I would argue, as cliché as it is, that every problem is an opportunity. That is, of course, if you're willing to maintain, as Dr. Jeff Spencer would call it, the Champion's Mind. And as such, the rest of the way I'll say "opportunity" rather than "problem."

Let's look at two examples:

1. Onboarding clients
2. Client retention

If we ran a marketing firm and applied I-learning, we would go and research how other marketing firms were approaching onboarding. Maybe we'd hire a marketing firm coach and try to glean what they'd done. We would probably look at marketing firm software related to onboarding. And so on. Then we'd ultimately select what we thought represented the so-called best practice. Hoorah, good job by us.

We implement the solutions.

And then we have all these issues. We look at the issues and realize: *Oh yeah, we aren't like most other marketing firms because we have several ways we differentiate our offers that aren't what a standard marketing firm does.*

So then what do we do? Go back to our research and

consider picking the second-place option? Or do we accept a broken system? We try to modify the solutions to fit our needs and do the whole square peg, round hole thing.

If we considered a T-learning approach, we could have said: Who does onboarding best? Not specific to our domain but generally as a concept?

Perhaps we conclude it's Southwest Airlines. They, in many ways, revolutionized onboarding.

Now we can explore how their onboarding process worked. What can we glean from that that applies to our business? What are the similarities and differences?

Then we could say, outside of industries, what are some social norms that are similar to onboarding? Well, how about dating?

What do we know about dating that would work really well if we wanted it to turn into a long-term relationship? We'd probably show up on time, listen more than we talked, not try to be someone we weren't, show them that we were interested and appreciate them.

What can we glean from this and apply to our business and onboarding?

From that, we find that as a service-based business where relationships are key, successful onboarding is more about maintaining the proper social norms. And if we violate social norms and treat someone like a market norm, there's really no going back. There is research from Dan Ariely's book, *Predictably Irrational*, that shows how once you violate social norms, you can't go back.

Now let's look at client retention. We could, of course, go back to other marketing firms and do *all* the research, but if the onboarding example teaches us anything, it's that we likely already have the answers.

Again, we have a service-based business. That means it's a relationship-centric business. And it turns out, we've maintained long-term relationships with friends and family. And we also know what causes a long-term relationship to sour.

We can look to social norms and ensure we don't violate them by treating the client with a market norm.

We can also look at things like IC-DISC, the Kolbe A Index or Love Languages. In other words, not every person is the same. In the Love Languages example, some clients want gifts and some want acts of service. The more we know about the client, the more we can meet them at their point of need. In other words, if you have a relationship with someone and it's not transactional, you can't treat them like everyone else.

The through-line between these two examples is that by breaking free from our domain, we can draw on insights we already have to leverage opportunities we encounter. We can also use it to anticipate future opportunities and design systems and processes accordingly.

Now, how do we practically implement this?

When faced with an opportunity, step one is to categorize the problem. In other words, what is the type of opportunity? Be as specific as you possibly can. I would typically have utilized the Professional Skeptic Frame here to keep digging deeper and challenging my assumptions.

Once we have the potential categories, step two is to come up with other industries, natural laws and social norms where you've observed the opportunity being solved already.

Step three is to then identify how the solutions work for your unique opportunity. Where are the gaps? Where are the similarities? Where do these solutions typically break? More importantly, will these solutions get me closer to the things I want?

Step four is to tailor the solution to your specific opportunity. We must ensure that we don't violate our Commandments. So we go back to customizing the solutions to ensure:

1. They will get us closer to the things we want (or at least not further away).
2. We don't get stuck on evaluating the solutions as if there's a right or wrong way.
3. We understand the financial consequences (the Four Lenses apply here).
4. We make sure we're making an asymmetric bet (the Four Lenses apply here as well).

The frequency that you'll utilize this approach is likely daily, if not multiple times per day. As a purpose-driven opportunity, there's no shortage of opportunities. The good news is if you practice this, it will become a habit, and when it becomes a habit, it will begin to happen on auto-pilot. You'll naturally label the opportunity and default to T-learning. It will become the default mode, whereas I-learning is likely your current default.

Rig the Game:

- You evaluate asymmetric risk by looking at your options through four different lenses: Time Savings, Forcing Function, Cost Savings/Reduction and Revenue Generator.
- When we water the weeds, we inadvertently take time and energy away from our priorities by supplementing obstructive structures in our business.
- Maximization often comes at the detriment of optimizing our priorities; the push for more leaves us further away from what we truly want in our business.

12

THE GROWTH PRINCIPLES

Although we are focused on analyzing our decisions to our best advantage and moving forward with a clear head, the fact remains that we still want to grow. The danger, however, when we talk about growth is that we can become awash with a "more" mindset and unintentionally be back on the hamster wheel getting further away from what we want. Consequently, I built these principles in a way that they force me to apply rigor. After all, the biggest risk is that I don't get what I want out of life.

These principles, when used in tandem, aid in applying all four of the Certainty Commandments:

1. **Rely on a Preponderance of Data.** A tool specifically designed to force us to stop us from acting off speculation.
2. **Bias Microsteps.** A tool designed to force us to take the smallest possible step so we get the data required.

3. **Consider the Rule of Three and 10.** A tool that reminds us of the next breakpoints in our business so we can plan accordingly.

4. **Only Scale at the Optimal Ratios.** A tool that reminds us that we might not be ready to scale and more might not be the answer.

Rely on a Preponderance of Data

Here's a little secret: learning to rely on a preponderance of data (rather than speculation), is key. Why? Because business owners (humans, really) *love* to speculate. The problem is that there's rarely any data to support the speculation.

We are going off our guts. We know things. We *feel* things. We learn to tune into instinct. And then we convince ourselves to burn the boats and gamble it all.

But unless we had a gambling problem to begin with, we wouldn't bet our life savings at the casino. (Remember we are all gamblers, right?)

Let's take taxes. People love to speculate on what Congress might or might not do. I've had some people put off forming 401ks, for example, because they've heard they might be eliminated from the tax code, only to miss out on years of contributions.

What do Bill Gates, Sara Blakely, Oprah Winfrey, Whitney Wolfe Herd, Meg Whitman, Elon Musk, Jeff Bezos and the aforementioned Fortune 500 companies all have in common besides absurd amounts of money?

They have a metric ton of data.

All of these household figures and organizations have an incredible amount of data on every bit of the market, their customers, manufacturing, engagement, you name it. Add the data they collect for themselves to the data that's readily available to illustrate buying and interest trends (or anything else you might need to know about), and by the time a decision needs to get made, there's very little speculation that needs to be done. Information gaps are few and far between.

And even though we, with our smaller organizations, maybe don't have the access or the information these larger operations have, the principle still stands. We have to take action and make decisions based on the data we can see rather than a speculative attitude of, "They bought from me before, so they'll buy from me again." In other words, we have to work with sample sizes of more than one or two.

If we don't happen to have enough data, then we go to our next principle.

Bias Microsteps

Large, expensive, magnificent marketing funnels seem like an attractive way to get attention and bring in clients and customers, but the reality is, our audience may not respond to a big, fancy funnel. So before we invest in a funnel like that, we want to see if our list could buy from an email instead. And if our list won't buy off of a series of emails, the funnel is almost definitely out.

We use microsteps to validate the assumptions we are making about the decisions we make in the marketer frame.

A microstep is a tactic that requires the least amount of effort and risk but leaves all the options open to get us the necessary data to proceed (to the next step). This requires us to think deeply about what the actual lead domino is in this scenario.

For example, if we think we have a new product idea that people will buy, we might ask, "What would need to be true in order for us to be certain that people want to buy it?"

Oftentimes, a waitlist of people waiting to buy is a good

indicator, so the microstep may be to put up a waitlist and promote it.

If the waitlist fills up with people eager to buy, that's validation that we can move forward with the cost of building out the next step. If nobody signs up for the waitlist, it's a sign that something about the offer is not as compelling as we had hoped, and it's a good thing we didn't put the time, effort, energy and other resources into a full product launch.

Now instead of building out everything else, we allocate our resources to either figuring out what needs to be done for people to sign up or a different opportunity.

And going along with the idea of making decisions based on a preponderance of data, the best way we can build up that data is to incrementally validate our understanding of things so that we can proceed effectively.

All these tools allow us to process issues and decisions the same way, through the same frames, which will allow us to opt in rather than opting out.

Remember, it is much harder to opt out than it is to opt in.

Consider the Rule of Three and 10

There is a cost that is inherent to building new things. Building new systems and infrastructures, upgrading software or hiring new people all have a cost associated with them.

This rule was invented by Hiroshi Mikitani, the CEO of Rakuten, the Japanese retailer, but I originally learned of it when former Evernote CEO Phil Libin was interviewed on a podcast some six or seven years ago.

The concept is that as your business grows, there are natural breakpoints. That is when the systems, policies, procedures, frameworks and software no longer work. Under the Rule of Three and 10, everything breaks whenever your business triples or hits an order of magnitude of 10. That is, three,

10, 30, 100, 300, 1,000. These breakpoints exist across all business units, departments, products and service lines.

Let's give the example of employees.

When it's just you, you can often get away with everything being very informal. You could potentially maintain your client population in a spreadsheet, be on your spouse's health insurance and not have any policies about when or how you work.

When you hire that second employee, you can tell them, "Look, you're my first employee. I don't have benefits set up, systems documented or other things formalized." That hiree, if reasonable, would not be surprised. If anything, they'd expect that to be the case.

But alas, we make the next hire. We are now a team of three. Now the feedback loops have loosened (hello, telephone game) and this business is growing. The need for formalized processes grows. The system (or lack thereof) is broken.

So what do we do? Well, you guessed it—it depends.

We must go back to our Commandments. I'm going to keep reminding you that every action must get us closer to what we want. In most things, there's no right or wrong. It's always a financial decision and we need to ensure we have more upside than downside.

If we consistently do these things, then we are rigging the game.

Let me expand on what this means on a practical basis.

If your desire is to have more time soon, it's probable that hiring more people will *not* achieve that priority. Take, for example, Brooks's Law. Created by Fred Brooks in his book *The Mythical Man,* Brooks's Law says "adding manpower to a late software project makes it later."

That means if we're at a head count of three but hiring more people will get us further away from our current goal, then we need to pause. That means we won't likely hit our next breakpoint within the year. This is a relevant data point to know. Will I hit the next breakpoint in a year or less?

My general default is that if there's a preponderance of data to suggest that we will reach the next breakpoint within the next year, then we will build to that level (in this example, 10). In the short term, we are knowingly opting into overbuilding to avoid a re-build in less than a year. Of course, we will utilize T-learning to arrive at a range of solutions and utilize the Four Lenses to create asymmetry. These algorithms work together. They aren't discrete in that regard.

When the timeline will exceed more than a year before we hit the next breakpoint, then we default heavily to the Four Lenses. Through the Four Lenses, are we creating substantial asymmetry by implementing it now?

Now back to what we're trying to get closer to—more time. We've established that, generally speaking, hiring more people will not get us more time, at least not in the short term. As such, we aren't going to reach 10 people in the next year. That means that absent an outcome from our Four Lenses analysis, we are going to build the system for three.

What this has done is multi-faceted and it's important you don't miss these subtle nuances.

This framework allowed us to avoid defaulting to "more." Our default tendency would have likely been to overbuild. We also tend to berate ourselves when we have to build a solution to an opportunity we've solved in the past. We might say things like:

I just did this two years ago; I can't believe I have to do this again!

Why didn't I anticipate these things?

I picked the wrong solution.

Or perhaps your business partner, significant other or employees level some scrutiny.

Didn't we just do this?

How did you not foresee this coming?

This approach instead allows us to create allegiance capital. Allegiance capital is the concept that you build loyalty among your following by telling them, at the right time, what will happen next.

For example, you would inform your followers: "We are going to build it as follows: When we reach 10 employees, we know we will need to rebuild the systems, processes and procedures. The data suggests that won't happen for more than a year and there's no asymmetry to overbuilding it now. I'm telling you this because we know this isn't the forever solution."

Conversely, you could opt to overbuild and in this case broadcast that as well. "Look, we know that we're going to have a system with features we aren't going to use. You might start questioning the choice or see the bill and think we are overpaying. We implemented this solution because the data indicated that if we didn't we would have to rebuild the system again in less than a year."

Lastly, I want to point out that this approach allows you much greater control over your finances. What I suggest is that quarterly, you evaluate your business segments, customer lists and employee projections to determine when you will reach the next breakpoint.

Based on those breakpoints, you can update your quarterly and annual action plans based on what opportunities need to be addressed. This breaks the loop of overpaying because you waited too long. When you wait too long, you pay the price twice—you pay the hard costs, which are generally more, *and* the cognitive burden that invariably ensues.

Imagine for a moment that you just brought on your third employee but expect to have 10 in just a few months. In this case, it may make sense to wait until you have 10 employees to rebuild your infrastructure, or overpay to prematurely build for 10, because it will still be cheaper than paying for a system that supports three and then quickly having to pay the cost of tearing it down and rebuilding it again for 10.

Armed with this knowledge, we can figure out the most efficient way to scale.

You heard right; you can actually go a long way toward predicting the rough patches your business may hit based on the Rule of Three and 10. And the value of knowing when these breakdowns in your systems or processes may happen is that you can prepare for them and opt into staff or structures that you'll be able to build up in advance of the anticipated breakpoint and rebuild ahead of the next one.

Only Scale at the Optimal Ratios

There's a false narrative that scaling is the solution to every problem. Often, I'll see a business that's unprofitable and their solution is that they just need to grow more. So they double down, hire more folks, add more revenue and find themselves in the same position—or worse.

The reality is that unless you're venture-backed and can grow through negative cash flow, having "more" is not going to be helpful. Simply relying on "more" is a false assumption that adds too much risk, often requires maximum effort and leaves you with limited options.

We all know that building a home on a shaky foundation is a recipe for disaster. Yet we're convinced that's the way to grow our business. It's frankly much easier to explain to your stakeholders that the business isn't failing, you just need a little bit more growth and that will fix all the problems.

Instead, because we know that we are biased and will default to "more," I recommend that we set targets or ratios in advance. I do this across all departments and businesses.

For example, if we launch a marketing campaign, what are the ratios we need to hit to call the campaign a success and justify ramping up spending? If we don't do this in advance, we easily fall victim to our marketing agency telling us the solution is to spend more so we get the data required.

As another example, let's consider operations. What is the client profitability per employee required? We set that target in advance because we know whenever we're busy, the recommended solution will be to hire more people. But we also know that each new hire is going to require four to five hours per week of oversight, and training them up might get us further behind on work. So if we're really busy and the profitability isn't within our range, we should first consider how to solve that problem. That might mean firing some clients, increasing fees or implementing new processes and systems.

I could continue with more examples, but the underlying message is that when we hold ourselves accountable to metrics in advance, we force ourselves to consider all the trade-offs. In turn, we create a dynamic where we can often get what we want out of our business without having to actually take on more work.

Rig the Game:

- In rigging the game in our favor, we must employ growth principles in order to stay above financial risk and ruin.
- An abundance of data outweighs speculation when it comes to making financial decisions and placing bets on the outcome.
- When we take microsteps, we can avoid potential ruin and actively manufacture the life and business we want.
- Though breakpoints generally exist as our business grows (the Rule of Three and 10), anticipating these obstacles puts us in charge of our own arena.
- We know we are biased and default to "more," so setting targets in advance helps us to ask the right questions before we build on an already shaky foundation.

"External things are not the problem. It's your assessment of them. Which you can erase right now."
—Marcus Aurelius

PART IV

RIGGING YOUR GAME

13

THE RULES OF RIGGING THE GAME

U p to this point, I've focused on the mental side of entrepreneurship. I've established the key Commandments and the Algorithms for decision-making.

The remainder of this book will be focused on the practical implementation of the concepts and principles so that we rig the game to win. This book is, after all, ultimately about how to get the outcome or outcomes that you want without having to compromise who you are. That is the essence, in my opinion of winning.

I must however caution you that the Human Mindset will creep in and you'll likely default to maximizing over optimizing. The human tendency is to think: *I have to finish this book and understand it entirely before I can implement any portion therein.* That is a great example of valuing maximizing over optimizing—we want to do it all now and if we can't we'll entirely arrest our progress.

Applying the Four Commandments and Algorithms, however, is a shift in your thinking. You will be creating new habits. Phenomenologically, many believe that it takes 21 days to form a habit. That data point comes from the book *Psycho-Cybernetics* by Dr. Maxwell Maltz. New data suggests, and this won't surprise you as a reader of this book, that it actually...depends.

A research article on Healthline.com appropriately titled "How Long Does It Take for a New Behavior to Become Automatic?" written by Scott Frothingham and medically reviewed by Timothy J. Legg, Ph.D., says:

"It can be anywhere from 18 to 254 days for a person to form a new habit and an average of 66 days for a new behavior to become automatic."

There's no one-size-fits-all figure, which is why this time-frame is so broad; some habits are easier to form than others, and some people may find it easier to develop new behaviors.

There's no right or wrong timeline. The only timeline that matters is the one that works best for you.

All that to say: we don't know how long it'll take to fully re-shift our thinking to align with the Four Commandments. That's perhaps the best possible argument for starting now!

And now that you've started, you're officially on the path towards rigging the game.

The next few chapters will break down the actual steps that make up the practical application of the operating system. Below is an overview of each step and how it maps to the Four Certainty Commandments.

1. **Playing Your Game**—This chapter covers how to figure out "your game" and the actions to take when you're out of alignment.
2. **Creating Your Solvable Problem™**—This chapter covers how to define what "you want" so you can effectively calculate whether you're getting closer or not.

3. **Closing the Gap**—This topic will cover multiple chapters and cover how to close the gap on your Solvable Problem™.

As you proceed, recognize that this game I refer to is infinite. You're not set for life after you figure out your game and your Solvable Problem™.

Rather, along the way, old habits might creep back in that cause you to play someone else's game. And as you make progress, your preferences will change and evolve. Consequently, your Solvable Problem™ will change along with the gap you're working to close. We need to honor and respect this infinite game.

That means that we give ourselves grace to evolve.

Shaming yourself because what you thought you wanted has changed doesn't serve you in getting "closer." In fact, that time you spend spinning out costs you valuable momentum.

That's why one of the greatest benefits of this operating system is not directly monetary. Rather, if in the past a setback spun you out for weeks and now it's days, you've improved beyond measure.

14

PLAYING YOUR GAME

Many entrepreneurs are told by their coaches or mentors to create a vision board in connection with finding their why. Now, I'm not against vision boards or the whole narrative around finding your why, *per se*. But I do find the approach simplistic at best and problematic at worst.

Let's go back to the beginning when we established *anxiety = uncertainty x powerlessness*.

For many (I'd actually venture to say most) entrepreneurs, the vision board and whole notion of their why create more anxiety. In fact, they are almost paralyzing.

Why don't I know my why? (That's uncertainty).

I have this vision board, but I don't know how I'm going to achieve it all. (That's powerlessness).

You've probably heard about the risk iceberg. The risk iceberg is the idea that above the surface, we find known knowns, but lurking below the surface is a much larger set of risks composed of known unknowns, unknown knowns and unknown unknowns.

That risk iceberg is floating in your mind when you start

contemplating your vision board and trying to articulate your why. The internal dialogue is some version of: *How can I possibly map out my manifest destiny when there's so much I don't already know?*

That's why my longtime mentor, Randy Massengale, says, "First we start with frequency (doing the work); from the frequency, we increase our intensity, and from our intensity, we find our purpose."

See, a few years back, I felt stuck. My accounting firm was growing and accumulating awards, but personally, I felt as if I kept losing momentum, getting knocked off my game and being in my own way. I reached out to a few friends looking for a suggestion for a coach or mentor and was referred to Randy Massengale.

Randy's 40-plus-year career has been spent in and around disruptive technology companies (some of which he founded) and education, both as a board member at Lewis & Clark College and Seattle University and as the author of numerous articles spanning topics related to academia and career/organizational development.

Long story long, Randy is a genius with decades of experience to prove it.

When I found myself at a career crossroads, he too told me to start with repetition.

But repetition of *what*?

This is where I learned the essence of playing your game.

See, a good coach builds a game plan to set up their star athletes to succeed. In your business and personal life, you're the coach and the most important player. So building a game plan that is not perfectly aligned to maximize your strengths and minimize your weaknesses is just another way to beat yourself.

Who are you? What's your style of business? What kind of game plan will allow you to show up as your best?

To figure out how to keep your pursuits aligned with your unique disposition, we need to combine a phenomenological archaeological dig with a more rigorous, objective process.

Subjective/Phenomenological: First, we need a process to perform a personal archaeological dig to figure out what our individual history of decision-making, successes and failures tells us about ourselves.

The most effective method for learning my personal style of play I learned from Randy.

This method starts with a few questions about the sport (or hobby) you loved growing up. Remember, detailed answers will be more helpful to you.

1. *What was your favorite sport or hobby growing up?* This *doesn't* have to be a sport or hobby that you played the most. It *does* have to be a sport or hobby that you felt the most aligned with as a kid. In other words, the sport or hobby that you felt the most passion toward.
2. *What about this sport or hobby did you enjoy?* Think about what it looked like. Were you part of a team or on your own? What were the sounds, textures and specific details about it that you loved so much?
3. *What was your style of play during this sport or hobby?* Perhaps you were a star player or more of a team player. Maybe you were incredibly fast and strong or showcased a particular skill or talent.

Once you've got the answers to those questions down on paper, it's time to consider how your answers relate to how you operate in your business. For that, we have a second set of questions.

1. How do your answers to the questions above compare/align with the way you operate in your business?
2. Do you operate in congruence with the way you played your favorite sport or hobby? If yes, how so? If not, why?
3. Do the things that give you the highest level of enjoyment in your business align with your favorite sport or hobby? If yes, how so? If not, why?
4. How can you operate more in congruence with the way you played your favorite sport or hobby?
5. Why would you be resistant to operating more in congruence? In other words, what are the downside risks?

The argument for why this works so profoundly is that as a kid, you largely got to figure out the sport or hobby you liked best and how you showed up and played. To some degree, then, the activity you chose (and how you participated) was the freest expression of who you are. As you progress through formal schooling, however, you tend to be forced to conform to a whole host of social norms and you often lose some of the things that you really enjoyed in that favorite sport or hobby because you're told you have to act in accordance with those norms.

But what I find universal, having done this exercise with numerous people, is that for folks who are acting in alignment with the way that they would play their favorite sport or hobby, it tends to be the greatest upside for them to lean into those attributes (hello, asymmetry to the upside).

And while putting all this down on paper allows you to play your game *more* and gives you the greatest potential for upside, it's also going to have the greatest potential for downside. Our greatest strength tends to be our greatest weakness. I know that much from experience.

For a personal example of this process, my favorite sport growing up was basketball. And what I really enjoyed about the sport is that, although you're on a team, you have the opportunity to be an independent contributor and you can somewhat dictate the outcome of the game. There's an opportunity to take the last shot.

See, I also wanted to be a shooting guard. I wanted to have the ball in my hand for the last shot, but sadly, I'm also not the most athletically gifted person. So hustle was also my thing.

The way that translates for me in business is that when I don't feel like I'm making an impact, when I'm just going along with what everyone else is doing, then I start feeling complacent. I want to be part of a team, but I also want to have the opportunity to make an impact in the game and I'm willing to take some risks.

Now the problem with that mindset is that sometimes, rather than taking the last shot myself, I need to pass the ball. Sometimes I don't need to hustle. So it becomes a little bit of a mental exercise for me to be able to step back and reflect and ask myself, "Am I playing my game *too much* here?" In other words, am I taking too many risks and do I need to pass the ball instead? That reflection, and the chance to recalibrate, is the thing that always helps me up-level my business.

Rigorous, Objective Process: Then we need to look at what a more rigorous, scientific process tells us about ourselves.

As far as figuring out who you are within your business and how to play your own game effectively, I favor the Kolbe A Index. Kolbe A is an assessment questionnaire, but it goes beyond giving you your basic personality type. This test is designed to help you identify your natural, instinctive strengths

—the things that make you *you*—which is a big help as you work to get aligned with the parts of your personality that affect how you operate within your business.

There are plenty of other approaches and assessments to help you answer these questions, but you also probably have some existing sense of who you are and how you operate as an entrepreneur.

Are you a visionary? A quick-start type of person? A fact-finder? How do you tend to make decisions? Do you jump in headfirst or take a more cautious approach?

What the Kolbe A provides is a score on each of these categories, specifically: Fact-Finder, Implementor, Quick Start and Follow-Thru. Having this quantified score gives you:

1. **A tool you can share with your teammates.** I've found that providing a rigorous, objective test along with your subjective/phenomenological assessment of your tendencies leads to a higher level of cohesion among teams.

2. **A tool you can use to add members to your team.** This tool can allow you to fill in the gaps of your team. For example, if you know you're high on Quick Start and low on Follow-Thru, you find someone that's a complement to you. Too often, we end up hiring off of what we like, and that might be more people who are like us, with the same skill set.

Remember: Your business exists to serve *you* as you are the GM, head coach and star player. You need to know your tendencies and preferences so that you have some context for the decisions you make to support and drive your business while consistently playing your game.

Any time we are playing a game other than *our* game with a style other than *our* style, we are unnecessarily swimming upstream—yet another unnecessary battle we wage against ourselves. We will inevitably get off course. The world will constantly tell us to be someone different.

When this inevitably occurs, we go back to frequency. That is, what is the one thing that you can do that represents the essence of playing your game? It could literally be the sport that you love. In my case, to get back on track with playing my game in life and business, the best thing I can do is go to the gym and put up some shots (that is a homework assignment Randy has given me). Over the course of days or weeks, I start to find a higher level of intensity that leads to clarity (what I need to do next).

In other circumstances, the best course of action is to review your time and commitments while asking yourself the question: Am I operating in congruence with the way I played in my favorite sport or hobby? If yes, how so? If not, why?

If you practice this consistently, over time you'll be able to catch yourself sooner before you commit to an action that will require you to play someone else's game.

Rig the Game:

- Frequency is the lead domino. It's through frequency that we find a higher level of intensity that ultimately leads us to finding purpose.
- There is no one-size-fits-all approach to establishing how you play your game; develop a personal strategy for success that supports your strengths as the most valuable player.
- Rigging the game in our favor is much more individualized than we may first assume and starts with who we are as a person rather than as an entrepreneur.

15

THE SOLVABLE PROBLEM™

The biggest risk, as I've reminded you throughout, is that we don't get what we want out of life. Avoiding that risk requires regularly evaluating what we want so we can align our actions with Certainty Commandment #1: Closer Over More.

Back in Chapter 4, when I covered Certainty Commandment #1 in detail, I established the impossibility of solving a multi-variable equation. That is, if I asked you to tell me the value of X in the equation $X + Y = 10$, your answer would be either unknown or infinity. Why? Because there is more than one unknown variable.

The multi-variable equation conundrum is also how we tend to approach what we want out of life. That is why we need what I call a Solvable Problem™. We have created a Solvable Problem™ when we've turned what we want into life, both tangible and intangible, into dollar values that have an assigned date to them (I want a $1M house in three years and I want five more hours of free time per week within a year at a cost of $5K per month).

Absent a Solvable Problem™, we can never answer the

question: *Do we need to make more?* And, if we don't know if we actually need to make more, then our tendency will be to default to "more" as the singular solution to our problems.

To give some context, a few years ago, I was putting together a presentation for an event and I sent the slides over to a few of my partners to get some feedback. Since I was sharing a stage with Daymond John (CEO of FUBU and an investor on *Shark Tank*), I wanted to knock this one out of the park. After getting feedback, I added one line (bolded below):

"Most people will never define personal success because in doing so, they also define failure. Once you've defined what actually matters to you, you can no longer hide behind all the vanity metrics."

See, for you to get what you truly want out of life, you have to define what really matters most. If what you really want is to be home for dinner and never miss your daughter's soccer game, then you're not successful until you're home for dinner and are attending every one of your daughter's soccer games.

Now, as it turned out, I triggered a lot of folks at that event. Everyone is accustomed to going to these events to get a dopamine boost and leave jacked up on 10X this and fix-your-mindset-bro that.

The Solvable Problem™ is the antithesis of that approach, and the method is designed only for those who are willing to go after what they actually want with the orientation of the least amount of effort and risk while leaving optionality. We can only achieve this through the willingness to define success (and therefore simultaneously define failure).

Now let's dig into the Solvable Problem™. The best way I've found to think about the Solvable Problem™ is by identifying it as your own personal definition of wealth. As it is your own, that inherently means that Certainty Commandment #2, about the difference between preference and binary, is strongly at play here. You will need to fight the tendency to create the *correct* Solvable Problem™. There isn't an answer key that will give you the correct Solvable Problem™.

That said, I've found that more often than not when I ask someone what they want, it's either accompanied with a blank stare or a list of things they feel they *should* want. As such, I've created a framework helping you to construct your Solvable Problem™ with two options (*note: I've created a web-based app called the CertaintyApp where you can use either option which can be accessed for free at www.CertaintyApp.com*).

Option 1 is the shortcut method. Under this method, you back-of-hand determine the total dollar amount you need to live the life that you want using the rule of four. The rule of four says that during any given year you don't want to use more than four percent of your liquid assets on expenses. As four percent x 25 = 100, you can take your current (or projected future) annual spending times 25 and add in any extra one-time expenses to reach your total Solvable Problem™.

For example, if I currently spend $300,000 after taxes per year and I expect to purchase a $1,000,000 house and pay off all my debt for $500,000, my Solvable Problem™ would be:

Step 1: $300,000 x 25 = $7,500,000
Step 2: $7,500,000 + $1,000,000 (house) = $8,500,000
Step 3: $8,500,000 + $500,000 (debt) = $9,000,000

If I then set a singular date to fund all of these priorities, I now have a Solvable Problem™. All I need to do now is look at how much I have in current assets and what extra cash flow I have per year and I can solve for the rate of return I need on my investments to achieve my Solvable Problem™. If I didn't find that return to be possible, then I could determine what I think is a more appropriate rate of return and solve for how much more I need to make. Then the question becomes: how do I achieve this with the least amount of effort, the least amount of risk and the most amount of options?

Option 1, the Shortcut Method, is the preferred method for those just getting started. Why? Because we optimize before we maximize. Just by establishing a high-level number, we can now begin to formulate the next steps without getting overwhelmed.

Eventually, as you make progress, you may want to refine it further as you recognize that not all priorities are created equal. One priority might be five times more important than the next and so on.

That leads me to Option 2: the Detailed Method. Under this method, we will break your Solvable Problem™ into its individual priorities so that we can assign each a dollar value and a date (the Shortcut Method assumes we achieve everything at once). To do this, this method takes your Solvable Problem™ and breaks it into two categories: Core Priorities and Preference-Based Priorities.

The Core Priorities are what I've found everyone seems to want (and, after going through this exercise more times than I can count, I've yet to have someone push back). There are three priorities under this category:

- **Paying Off Debt**—having enough funds to pay off any current debt.
- **Funding Retirement**—having enough funds to not have to work. It doesn't mean you don't continue to work. Rather, you have options.
- **Reserves**—some additional capital earmarked for the unexpected so you don't have to tap into the funds for debt and retirement.

To get momentum on creating your Solvable Problem™, I

suggest everyone start with these three. The task at hand is to assign a dollar value to each priority and the date you'd like to fund it.

As I said earlier, there's no correct Solvable Problem™, as your core priorities are unique to you. Perhaps you've already funded one or more of the priorities. Further, the amount of debt, required funds for retirement or required reserves are unique to your preferences past, present and future, just as the timeline for when you want to achieve funding these priorities is unique as well. As an example, perhaps you experience a lot of cognitive burden around debt and consequently desire a shorter timeline to pay off the debt than is required by the lender.

That's a preference.

Just understand that in doing so, we need to invoke Commandments #3 and #4 and acknowledge that there are trade-offs to paying off debt sooner and it may not be asymmetric to the upside relative to all other options.

Once you lock in your Core Priorities, you can pause and celebrate.

Then, move on to the second category: Preference-Based Priorities. These are the priorities that are unique to you. Below is a list of examples. You have the freedom to list whatever you want. It is your life after all. The objective ultimately is to assign a dollar amount to each (what it costs) and a date (when you want to achieve it).

Examples of Family-Oriented Priorities:
Going on vacation every year with your family
Paying for your kids' college education or travel sports team
Retiring your parents or your spouse
Spending more time with your kids on the weekends

Examples of Personal-Oriented Priorities:
Sleeping better at night
Having more free time to yourself
Buying a dream car or home you've always wanted

Examples of Priorities Oriented Around Hobbies and Goals:
Going to every Seahawks game every year
Having time to golf, go fishing or participate in another hobby
Finally writing that book

The reason these priorities are so tricky is because there is no universal right or correct answer. You can't Google, "Should I want to go on vacation with my family?" or, "Should I grow my business?" and get an answer that is correct for everyone.

To bring back an earlier example, someone might ask: "Should I hire a nanny or an admin first?"

Once again, it depends on what your priorities are. Two people could have the exact same business of the same size in the same industry, but they will probably have different *preference priorities*. That's why the concept of relative priority is so important. You might have two priorities at odds with each other.

If they have an equal weight, you'll spin yourself in circles. However, if one priority is twice as important, then allocate resources accordingly. While operating in maximize mode (rather than optimize), we tend to treat priorities as if they are of equal importance—or worse, prioritize things that have little importance relative to what we want.

Now back to the nanny or the admin. One person may have determined that spending time with their kids is five times more important than growing their business. In which case, hiring a nanny and continuing to do their own admin work would get them further away from their priority—but not understanding the relative importance of those options leads to analysis paralysis.

Suffice it to say, identifying our Preference-Based Priorities and determining the relative priority is designed to help you find the most efficient path toward what matters most to *you.* Remember, the goal of this methodology is to get you to a place where you are both financially secure *and* happy. If you are not optimizing for your own priorities, you are not running your own race.

And no one wins a race they don't want to be in.

The other major advantage of knowing both your core priorities and your preference priorities is that it serves as a form of "sucker proofing."

Unless you live under a rock, you are surrounded each day by people who would love nothing more than to sell you their stuff. With each sales pitch comes a promise. A young, ambitious, slick, enterprising salesperson might swear that their product will give you more clients—a course that sells like crazy or an android clone with the beach body of your dreams with no workout needed!

But without a sense of what's important to you, both as a person and as a business owner, you might look at these claims and think, "Neat! Sounds good to me," and follow after the aforementioned salesperson. Fast-forward a bit, and you're in over your head with client fulfillment, running a course you never really wanted or stuck with an android for no reason at all.

If you've got a strong set of priorities based on goals and values that are important to you, you're equipped to look at the things you're being sold each day and instead consider whether that they line up with your Solvable Problem™, *and therefore whether those goals are going to get you closer to or further from what you actually want.*

The goal is not to have more stuff; it's to be wealthy. But what does wealth mean to you?

Core Priorities + Preference-Based Priorities = Solvable Problem™ (Your Personal Definition of Wealth)

You could probably get a different definition from Merriam-Webster, but your *personal* definition of wealth is the only one we're concerned about. Identifying your Solvable Problem™ and the preferences and reasons behind it will ensure that every move you make gets you closer to that all-important, personal version of wealth.

As I said earlier in this chapter, in my experience, very few people will ever do this, because they don't want to define success and failure.

But, there's also a second more nefarious reason why very few people will ever create their Solvable Problem™—they don't believe it could be that simple. And it is simple. But simple does not equal easy.

Maximize mode will creep in as soon as you start this process. You will get bogged down in the granular details and spun out when you think about trade-offs. You'll also have resistance due to the perceived commitment you're making to your Solvable Problem™.

The commitment is not, however, to the exact Solvable Problem™ you create today but rather to the willingness to change your Solvable Problem™ when new information arrives.

Ten years ago, I had an idea of what I would need to support a comfortable retirement based on what my spending habits and life looked like at that time. Over the subsequent years, my lifestyle and spending habits naturally shifted. This meant that what I needed to fund my Solvable Problem™ had changed. Like all things looked at in a realistic frame of mind, the things you value, the resources you have to support them and even the timeline, will shift. Allow them to do so. Assign each priority a date and dollar value based on what you have, what you want and what you know at the present moment.

Once you have all your priorities listed and properly sequenced based on relative priority, it's time to take action. Looking at your existing assets. You may be able to lock in your top priority or priorities, but in doing so there's a gut check that happens.

You've heard of putting your money where your mouth is. This step, which I call voting with your money, will be a big moment of truth in terms of figuring out what your *real* priorities are and whether they look different than the idealized future you have in your mind where no real resources are at stake.

I once had a client with whom I went through this exercise, and they listed their priorities in this order:

1. Pay off the farm
2. Buy more horses for the farm
3. Move to California

When we looked at their existing situation, they had enough cash flow at that moment to pay off the farm and buy the additional horses they wanted, but not to do all three.

When I told them this, it came to light that they were not willing to fund the first two priorities right now, which meant (gut check) *those were not actually their top priorities.*

If you're not willing to put your existing cash flow toward your top priority, it is not your priority.

This is a crucial step in the process because if we keep espousing one set of values but behaving from another—guess what? We are, again, fighting against ourselves.

We sat down and helped this client reorder their priorities, and they opted to make the move to California instead. We wound up with a list that looked different than the one we had when we started, but that's okay because it got them closer to what they actually wanted.

This doesn't mean that this client was wrong or misguided. It just means that when we applied real, existing assets to their priorities, we arrived at a more truthful and accurate picture of the way those priorities ought to be ordered. Which is, ultimately, what we want.

At the end of the day, it's crucial to get clear on your priorities and their order of importance so that your actions can match up with your desires. Otherwise, the more money you make, the more dissonance you create and the more your financial anxiety grows.

Rig the Game:

- You need a Solvable Problem™ to properly assess if you're taking actions that get you closer to what you want.
- When you're first getting started, use the Shortcut Method so that you can gain momentum (remember, first we optimize).
- Once you have momentum, apply the Detailed Method so you can sequence your priorities based on relative priority.
- Relative priority will be the key to determining how to allocate your resources.
- Understand that your Solvable Problem™ will evolve and the true relative priority can be revealed when you vote with your money.

"The future isn't a place that we're going to go. It's a place that you get to create."
—Nancy Duarte

PART V

CLOSING THE GAP

16

PUTTING IT ALL TOGETHER

So far we've covered the three things that separate the winners from the losers. Then we covered The Four Commandments, The 12 Principles, playing your game and the Solvable Problem™. The through-line of each of these sections is simple—*you!*

This system is about you.

What you want.

And leaning into your unique disposition.

It's not about becoming someone else.

The Commandments and Principles are all designed to help you figure out what you want so you get closer to what actually matters.

And because this system is about you, the best way to rig your own game is to start with what you already have. That is to say, if we can recover existing resources and reallocate them toward your Solvable Problem™, that inherently achieves our objective of the least amount of effort, the least amount of risk and the most amount of options.

When we talk about "existing resources," we aren't exclusively referring to money. There are other currencies: time, influence, energy and relationships (at a minimum).

When we examine these currencies, we tend to default back to cognitive distortions like all-or-nothing thinking such as:

- *I have recovered all of my time or it wasn't worth it.*
- *Either I feel fully energized or what's the point?*
- *This relationship is meeting all of my expectations or I'm going to burn it down.*

It's this type of thinking that could cause us to stop working with a coach, mentor or therapist. We find that we are still feeling some anxiety and conclude that the mentorship wasn't worth it. All of our pressures, fears and worries haven't disappeared after one or two therapy sessions, so what's the point? However, if we examine the problem closer, we might realize the following:

- *A year ago (before coaching or therapy) I was 80 percent more anxious.*
- *In the past, I would have made a decision that got me further away from what I wanted, and it would have taken two years for me to identify the problem, but now I identify it in a matter of weeks.*
- *I would get spun out over issues with partners, employees or clients and would ruminate on it for weeks, and now I'm able to course correct in hours.*
- *I understand better what triggers my anxieties and fear, and while I cannot prevent these things from happening, I know how to prepare for and handle them better now.*

This is progress! This is closer to the ultimate goal. The all-or-nothing thinking, overgeneralizations, tendencies to magnify issues and other cognitive distortions can lead us to focus on the negatives and miss that our relative improvement has been significant and perhaps life-changing.

All of this is to say that closing the gap by applying these principles does not mean that you won't experience failure, anxiety or shame. That would be designing a system that expects you to operate at your best at all times. Instead, we are designing a system that often allows us to prevent bad things from happening—and when they do happen, because they inevitably will, we can course-correct faster.

Through course-correcting faster, we can recover and reallocate resources sooner, which in turn allows us to get what we want sooner in the form of our Solvable Problem™.

That means that without thinking explicitly about recovering and reallocating money, you've already begun closing the gap by implementing the Certainty OS. You're recovering from poor decisions faster, which allots you more time, influence, energy and/or reputation. Put simply, you've raised the floor. By raising the floor, you've made it easier to touch the ceiling. Too often, we only want to raise the ceiling (focusing on more).

How "Less Is More" Can Get You Closer to Your Goals

Despite showing you the value of preventing or recovering from bad things, chances are you're still left with: *Yeah, but now what?* Perhaps, you might even be feeling a rising sense of anxiety. After all, by defining success, you've also put down what failure looks like (not funding what you've defined in your Solvable Problem™). The tendency is to default to "more" as the solution to quell this rising anxiety.

Before you take action and start loading up your plate with action items, take a pause. While you might not feel it at this moment, you've put yourself in a powerful position. By doing the work to define your Solvable Problem™, you can now calculate the gap. It would look something like this:

On the line in the image above, the second point represents the amount of resources you need to fund your Solvable Problem™ and the first point stands for the resources you have to allocate toward your Solvable Problem™ right now. Now we've got to address the space between the gap.

More specifically, because a lot of your priorities will have far-off dates attached to them, you'll need to answer the following question: Do you need to make more per year to fund your Solvable Problem™?

This is something of a trick question for a lot of people, mostly because they don't understand the power of compound interest.

Over the years I've spent working through this methodology with my clients, everyone assumes the answer is to increase the amount of money they make. Believe it or not, that is typically not the case. Usually, it's a matter of maintaining what you already make, which is an entirely different discussion.

What we often see is that once the dollar value and timeline of each priority are determined, given the current trend, the business owner is on track to fund their priorities in an appropriate timeframe. This means that taking on "more" is not the answer, because with more comes increased risk. Instead, it's about certainty.

Any moves made in this case should not be in the name of taking on more. They should be in the name of removing risk so that the trend continues and you get to what you want in the timeframe you have determined appropriate. In short, if you are *not* currently on track to fund your priorities in the appropriate timeline, you may need more cash. However, if you are on track, you *do not* need to improve revenue and cash flow. You just need to remove risk.

Unless we've mapped out what we're trying to reach, when we want to reach it, how much money we'll need to support it and how that amount differs from what we've got right now, there are too many open variables to be able to solve for "more," whatever that may be.

As we have seen throughout this book, focusing on more of a thing can get us farther away from what we actually want. After going through these exercises, we now have a measurement that has more utility to us: the gap. Every decision we make should close the gap between where we are and where we want to be.

In pursuit of "more" as the singular solution to solve all of our worldly problems, a nefarious thing unintentionally happens: We metaphorically step over dollars to pick up pennies.

Small business owners are notorious for having unused assets lying around: videos, articles, unused email lists, decommissioned products that could be repurposed and so on. Instead of utilizing these assets we already have (recovering and reallocating resources), we build new assets entirely from scratch. We step over dollars (the existing assets) to pick up pennies (start a new project from scratch with no data to support that it will be a success).

Think about it: If you want to generate more revenue, chances are you already have all the content you need. Perhaps it's about taking that content and translating it into a podcast, a webinar, a digital course, a lead generation magnet or even an e-book. The content you create can be used to generate new interest and business.

If you continuously put more time and attention into your existing assets, you will find more valuable content to share. You will save time and money and potentially avoid hiring an agency or other specialist to create shiny, new content. It's not always about shiny and new. Intentional and deep are just as important, especially when it comes to existing assets.

Multi-millionaire Brooke Castillo, who runs The Life Coach School, a 20-million-dollar-plus company, has gotten there by repurposing her material in a variety of ways. She has a monthly membership. She has a podcast. She does coaching calls. She creates premium events. She *never, ever* talks about new concepts. Her work is based on feelings, emotions and thoughts. Because her work is evergreen, she doesn't create new content. Instead, she consistently puts out what she calls B+ work because it's the work that matters: the overall concept. She knows her content is so strong that she doesn't need anything brand-new; instead, she utilizes all existing materials to drill results and boost ROI.

She has grown with what she already has, not what she continuously creates.

Small business owners are also notorious for having leaky buckets. Imagine trying to fill the kiddie pool with water. The faucet is 50 feet from the pool and we are using a bucket with several holes drilled in the bottom. By the time we get from the faucet to the pool, 80 percent of the water is gone. Unless you're a masochist, you'd take one trip and realize you need to patch the holes or find a new bucket. In entrepreneurship, we have a never-ending list of leaky buckets that largely go unmended:

→ We have sales funnels that collect email addresses, but we don't segment the data in any meaningful way to allow us to follow up accordingly.
→ We attempt to target early adopters with strategies that would only attract laggards.
→ We try to double our revenue so that we can double our profits. Meanwhile, we're completely ignoring our rising labor costs and idle staff.

→ We have software as a service on autopay that we have not utilized in years.

→ We have all of our money in one bank account yielding us .1 percent.

These are all examples of leaky buckets that cause us to do unnecessary additional work.

Say you have a business with $100,000 in revenue and a profit of $10,000. How could you double our profits?

Well, most of us would focus on more: We need *more* clients so we can have more revenue. The lead domino is that we either don't understand customer lifetime value or we've been too transactional with clients to have the relationships necessary to continually generate more work. So we will try every coaching program and paid advertising strategy on the planet to double our revenue to $200,000 so that we have $20,000 in profits.

Say we zoom out even further to incorporate our overall cash flow picture. Imagine our business is now doing $300,000 in revenue and after taxes, we put $150,000 in our pocket. How could we increase our cash flow from $150,000 to $200,000?

Again, my experience and the data say that most of us will focus on revenue. Since you've read the initial example, you might also consider expense reduction as a strategy.

There is, however, at least one other consideration: What if we reduced our tax bill and then reinvested those savings into an asset that produces additional tax deductions and income? In the US, for example, the federal income tax system is behavior-based. Meaning, if you changed your behavior, you could access some additional credits and deductions. So we could potentially close our entire cash flow shortage without having to either increase revenue or decrease expenses.

For example, for tax optimization, you work backward from

your Solvable Problem™. Ask yourself: What are the things I want to fund?

Then we examine the last three years' worth of returns because that's how far back we can go to amend. Can we get any money back?

Next, we examine your books. Is everything coded correctly to maximize deductibility (in the prior years, some meals were 100 percent deductible, but they weren't coded correctly so are they all being limited to 50 percent)?

Then we examine your entity structure (partnership, S-corp, C-corp, sole prop) and look at tax credits and deductions. What are we missing (leaky buckets) and what behavioral modifications can we make to save more? Where can we look at protective elections and proper reporting to minimize risk?

Finally, we get angry at our prior CPA for how much money they left on the table.

Luckily, there are strategies and solutions we will break down to think about tax optimization and provide some evergreen strategies for your consideration.

It all goes together.

Stop the Leaky Bucket With Resources You Already Have

Knowing where to look to save money is just as important as preventing overspending by applying the parenting frame, whereby we implement controls that allow us to opt into what happens rather than always having to opt out. Most of us have designed our financial systems where we have to opt out—we already spent the funds and now we have to ask for a refund or cancel so we don't get charged again.

In the chapters that follow, we will explore how to apply the Certainty OS to re-engineer your cash flow to achieve your desired profits without adding more effort or risk and without decreasing optionality.

As you proceed through these chapters, implement. Don't just read through them and think, "Huh, that sounds interesting." If you want to rig your own game, if you want to win, if you want to value "closer" over "more," then you must implement. No amount of reading, researching, taking courses or hiring gurus will help if you don't implement each and every principle and rule.

I promise if you implement these strategies and see for yourself how much additional cash you'll keep without having to do *more*, you'll be able to fund your goals—period.

That is, after all, the point, right? How we can get closer to our goals without doing more or taking on more risk while still playing our game?

17

CASH FLOW ENGINEERING

I've lost track of the number of calls with business owners who have said some version of "I know I need a budget and forecast." I used to agree, send them an agreement and my CPA firm would build them out a budget and forecast. A forecast, if you're not familiar, can take many shapes. You could do, for example, a revenue forecast and project what you expect sales to be every month. You could forecast expenses. You could forecast paying down debt.

What most entrepreneurs mean when they say forecast is they want a projection of cash flow, and that requires incorporating everything that goes on the Profit and Loss Statement and Balance Sheet: revenues, expenses, asset purchases, paying off debt, owner distributions.

We'd build out these projections and then the business owner would never look at them again. When I'd press them on this phenomenon, they'd reveal that they didn't see any meaningful value in the projections because the numbers were all basically guesses and the forecasts were no longer accurate days after completion.

Small businesses are different from big corporations. *Duh. Thanks, Dan.*

As you learned in the algorithms section, big corporations typically have a preponderance of data necessary to make the forecasts meaningful.

They also have the resources to maximize in that the forecasts are built by finance and accounting people *for* finance and accounting people.

Small businesses rarely have the preponderance of data necessary to forecast any area of their business, don't take the necessary microsteps to gather it and need to optimize rather than maximize.

As a consequence of this, rather than fight against reality, we must develop a new set of tools.

As a sidebar, in 2019, I predicted a recession was forthcoming and offered a live course called "Recession-Proof Your Business." Before building out the course, I took the first microstep and shared the idea on social media. After being called an idiot (that's the edited version) by many, I sold out the program. Those sales then justified taking the next step to build out the course.

Strangely, however, there were just a couple of attendees during week one and then none thereafter. After the second week of no attendees, I reached out to all the registrants to find out why they weren't showing up. Maybe it was a tech failure and they weren't receiving the emails?

Nope. They didn't believe a recession was forthcoming and they just bought the course because they wanted to support me. Blush. Well isn't that...nice?

Sadly, in my attempts at marketing, I didn't properly articulate the value of the program: it wasn't really about recessions. It was about the *steps you should take* to make your business as recession-proof as possible so that when a recession does happen (as it always eventually will), you can go on offense.

Knowing that I had an asset in place, I rebranded and slightly re-tooled the program as Cash Flow Engineering.

Cash Flow Engineering is a systematic process I developed to apply the Certainty OS you've been reading about in this book.

As you know, our optimal orientation is towards the least amount of effort, the least amount of risk and the most amount of options. As cash flow is often incredibly volatile —it's up for a few months and then suddenly it crashes—we need a process to recover and reallocate resources so that in all seasons of our business and the economy, we are getting closer to what we want.

To do this, I created an acronym: CASE. We need to first Compile. Then Analyze. Then Strategize. Then Execute.

In that order. Every. Single. Time.

Most of us just want to strategize or we just want to execute. Say the weekend comes and we come up with a laundry list of ideas while we are seeking dopamine. That was us just strategizing. But then Monday comes and we don't do anything with the list. Or we come in Monday and just start doing a bunch of stuff. That was us just executing. The danger is that we never compiled and then analyzed the data. And, as such, the strategy and/or execution might be entirely flawed.

I've used this analogy before, but it's consistently so relevant that I'm going to say it again: Google Maps will always give you directions. But if you enter at the wrong starting or ending point, the directions are irrelevant. We like to strategize, but we skip compiling and analyzing to accurately understand our true current position.

C: Compile

So what is compiling? If you're like most entrepreneurs, you read that word and were immediately triggered. "Nope, I don't

want to do this." Using Kolbe A scores as a proxy, I find entrepreneurs tend to be low on fact-finding (details). We want to be
visionaries, so we gloss over the details and jump straight to
strategizing and executing.

So, do me a favor and slip on a comfortable pair of your
Professional Skeptic Frames. When we compile, we are acting
with mindful intent to gather all the relevant data that we need
to do a complete analysis.

One of my best friends and longtime business partner in
Nth Degree CPAs, Nolan Bradbury, gave me a great analogy a
few years ago on the idea of intent. I now call it the Halloween
Candy Principle. On Halloween, what are the kids really trying
to accomplish?

On the surface, we might say "to eat as much candy as
possible." If you work in an office, you know about a week after
Halloween, parents start bringing in all the uneaten candy.
Sure, the parents may have reined in the candy consumption,
but kids also tend to forget about the Halloween haul a few
days later anyway. In other words, it's not about the candy. It's
about dressing up, acquiring the candy, comparing the candy
and then eating some.

If it were just about eating candy, we would run to the
grocery store and load up (or wait until a few days later and
load up on the discounted candy). That would, however, defeat
the whole point (Dad, where's the fun in just buying the candy
at a discount?!). To bring this full circle then, the Halloween
Candy Principle just establishes that we need to be really clear
on our intended outcomes.

Fortunately, we have a system to remind us of our intended
outcomes.

Are we getting closer to the things we want (our profit priorities) while acknowledging our preferences (and biases) so that
we consider all the trade-offs and make asymmetric bets to the
upside? To address that question, you need to compile a lot

more data than you're probably accustomed to when analyzing your finances. Take a deep breath—you can do this. Also, you have to.

As you gather this data, you will need to regularly ask yourself:

Is the data complete?
Is the data accurate?
Is the data presented correctly?
Is the data covering the correct period of time?
Is the data relevant?

After you answer each question, apply the Professional Skeptic Frame again and ask yourself: If I showed this information to my mentor, business partner, accounting partner, spouse or staff, would they align with me? If not, what questions would they pose?

The categories of information you'll want to compile when engineering your cash flow, at a minimum, are:

1. Your Solvable Problem™
2. Revenue data
3. Marketing data
4. Customer data
5. Employee data
6. Expense data
7. Asset data
8. Liability data

As I've established, our default tendency is to think "more" is the solution when, in fact, more could be disastrous in some circumstances. Revenue, Marketing, Customer and Employee data, in particular, tend to cause us to default back to "more" again. For the sake of this book, and considering there are already countless books on those topics (plus God only knows how many marketing-related coaches and consultants you've already worked with), I'm going to focus on expense data. That also tends to be the highest upside short term to recovering and reallocating resources.

If you want the full details on how I compile all the areas above, you can check out my full course at:

www.riggingthegame.com/cfe

With that said, let's dive into compiling expense data. The first step I take in compiling expense data is to pull the last 12 months of expenses summarized by the vendor. This is a report that you can run from most every accounting system. If the accounting system you are using does not have this report, check to see if there's an upgrade option and then, if necessary, change the software. This is a report available in QuickBooks, Xero and any more robust accounting solution.

You may be wondering:

Why sort by vendor rather than by expense type?
When we look by expense type, it summarizes all the individual transactions, but we need to look at the details in a more micro-level.

Why for the last 12 months rather than the previous year?
When we look at expenses based on the previous year, it does not fully account for changes we've implemented recently. As such, I almost always default to using rolling 12-month windows for reviewing data rather than calendar years. Business and life are not so simple to think every decision so neatly falls into calendar years and quarters.

Once I have the vendor report out of the accounting system, I paste the columns, including the vendor name and amount, into a Cash Flow Engineering spreadsheet that includes all the columns of metadata I want to compile about each line item. This spreadsheet is available at:

www.riggingthegame.com/resources

I'll describe each of the terms herein. To put you at ease, all the following terms will be utilized in the Analyze and Strategize steps in our process.

Frequency. How often does this expense occur throughout the year? Is it daily, weekly, monthly, bi-monthly, quarterly, annual or one-time?

Behavior. Is this expense fixed, variable, fixed-step or variable-step? A fixed expense is an expense that remains constant. A variable expense is an expense that's amount changes based on some driver (per product, per customer, per employee). A step cost represents that the amount will change (step up or down) after a specific event occurs.

For example, if all your employees are on salary, that would be a fixed cost. If when sales go from $50,000 to $75,000 per month, you know you'll need to hire more help, then that expense is fixed-step: the amount goes up by a fixed amount upon a specific action.

Similarly, say you produce 10,000 widgets per month and the average materials cost $.50 per widget. When your production gets to 15,000 widgets per month, you expect the average material costs to decrease to $.40 per widget. This would be an example of a variable step.

<u>Type</u>. What is the nature of this expense? Is it labor, software, service or a product?

<u>Usage Rate</u>. How often are you utilizing this expense in your business? In other words, we are distinguishing between how often we incur the expense (frequency) to how often it gets used. For this category, I look at the following: one-time, daily, weekly, monthly, bi-monthly quarterly, annually, perpetually and episodically (random or infrequent).

<u>Associated Savings.</u> Many of us incur an expense because we've rationalized that it will save us money or time. Enter your expected annual savings. If you don't have an expected annual savings, then enter zero.

<u>Savings Type</u>. If you entered an associated savings, what is that amount based on: hard cost, time-savings, avoidance cost or opportunity cost? A hard cost represents a dollar-for-dollar savings in a specific area of your business (rent, salaries, supplies). A time-savings represents the value of time saved in the specific area of the business this expense relates to, such as employee time (or, even better, your time!). An avoidance cost represents an expense you would have incurred if you didn't have this vendor in place (you have an outsourced IT manager and that saves you from hiring a full-time IT staff). Lastly, an opportunity cost, in this context, represents an expense that allows you to generate a gain from other areas of your business.

<u>Monthly Average</u>. This is a calculation field where we convert the expense amount to monthly. This is necessary because we have many different frequencies (monthly, quarterly, annual), and to analyze the data later we need the numbers to be comparable.

Effective Monthly Cost. This is also a calculation field where we convert the annual associated savings to monthly and subtract it from the Monthly Average field.

Month Added. When you originally began incurring this expense, in what month was it added?

Core. This is a yes-or-no field. Is the expense essential (core) to the operations of the business? In other words, if it were removed, could the business still operate without an impact on the quality of the product or service?

Segment. In what area of the business is this expense utilized? It could be marketing, sales, HR, accounting, a specific product or a specific segment. I would start with mapping out all the segments within your business. Separately, you will review each segment for the Rule of Three and 10. Remember, that rule says that whenever an area of our business triples or hits an order of magnitude of 10, everything breaks. Record for each business segment whether you expect any segment to hit the next breakpoint within the next 12 months.

Longevity. How long has your business been incurring this expense? I select less than a year, between one and three years or more than three years.

Relationship Type. What is the relationship you have with this vendor? Is it relational or transactional? Relational means you have a real relationship with the business or members of the team. Transactional means you pay them for a product or service but it's really just an exchange of money.

A: Analyze

Alright, now take a deep breath (yes, another one). You've done the compiling and now you're in a place to analyze the data. When we analyze the data, we will first start with the Professional Skeptic Frame.

The Professional Skeptic is looking for trends. You aren't coming up with solutions at this stage. We will find solutions in the Strategize phase. Remember, we need to be intentional about keeping these steps separate.

What you'll do next gets a little technical if you're not familiar with Excel or spreadsheets, but I assure you that via a few Google searches or at CFEClass.com, you can get up to speed on this without becoming a CPA or finance major.

Select the entire range of data in your spreadsheet. That is, select all the columns starting with vendor name and across to the last field, relationship type. Now insert a pivot table. A pivot table is a tool to summarize data. You can create a pivot table and keep changing the variables or you can create multiple pivot tables.

The desired outcome is to find any trends. The purpose is not, at this point, whether they are good or bad trends; rather, we are trying to get to the essence of the rhythm of our business, how we are or are not conforming to the industry rhythms and if our personal rhythms are having any impact.

Working through the data, now I'll start with frequency and work across to type.

Are the majority of our expenses monthly, quarterly or annual? Or is there no consistency across the frequency of our expenses? Either one might explain the cash flow roller coaster you've been on.

Are there any trends around the behavior of our expenses? Have we calculated our contribution margin? If we have a lot of step costs, are we prepared for the next step up?

As an aside, the contribution margin shows us how much we need to generate in sales to break even. To calculate the contribution margin, you take revenue per sale minus the variable costs per sale. The difference represents your contribution margin. Now that you have this number, you can divide your total fixed costs by the contribution margin and the output of that number is the amount of sales you need to break even.

Regarding usage, is there any disconnect between the frequency of the expense and how often we utilize the resource? This might also explain the volatility we're experiencing in our cash flow if we have a large disconnect between when we pay for something and when we actually utilize it in our business.

When we analyze annual savings, we're keying into a few trends:

1. What percentage of costs have no associated savings?
2. Is there a trend for the type of savings we've selected?
3. Are there any expenses that were not marked as core that also do not have an associated cost savings?
4. Are we realizing the cost savings on any expense where the cost savings was time-related? Is the business operating at full capacity to indicate that conclusion is accurate?
5. Is there a type of savings that we've selected that also correlates to a specific month when the expense was added?

We also specifically want to key into summarizing expenses by month added.

1. Are there any trends that are related to the rhythm of the industry, business or your personal rhythm? Perhaps you always add expenses that you believe will generate time savings after the industry's busy season. Or maybe you're like me in January, so you tend to add a lot of expenses because you're looking for shiny objects.
2. Remember the highest month paradigm? Is there any correlation between when you added expenses and your revenue?

As you look at trends around each business segment, key in on the following:

1. Are there any segments with no associated expenses?
2. Are there expenses overly concentrated to any specific segments (if I had to bet, it would be marketing)?
3. Are there any concentrations of expenses to a segment where we expect the Rule of Three and 10 to apply in the next year?

As you examine longevity, consider it in tandem with the relationship type:

1. Are a lot of your expenses under one year? Is this an indication of the highest month paradigm at play?
2. For relationships that are greater than one year, what percentage are relational versus transactional? Further, what about greater than three years?

As you've worked your way through these questions, hopefully, it's been eye-opening for you. Hopefully, the reaction is: In pursuit of more, I've made a lot of bets that haven't paid off. As well as:

- *Wow, now I can see why there's so much volatility in my cash flow!*
- *Wow, the highest month paradigm really got me this year!*
- *Wow, I always add expenses in July because I want more free time for the summer!*
- *Wow, I have a lot of expenses where the Rule of Three and 10 will apply soon, and I'm not at all prepared for that. Maybe that's why I'm always overpaying to fix problems.*
- *Wow, I have a lot of expenses that I don't consider core and also don't have associated cost savings! Maybe I should cancel them?*
- *Wow, there are months when I add expenses and they also happen to always be my lowest revenue months!*
- *Wow, it seems like I'm subject to (insert biases and cognitive distortions) more during this time of year or in relation to this specific segment of my business.*
- *Wow, I have a lot of software expenses that I pay monthly, but the usage is very infrequent!*

Now, ideally, you also compiled data about the other categories I discussed above (revenues, customers, employees). This data would allow you to look at expense trends in relation to each category.

S: Strategize

Strategizing is the world entrepreneurs like to spend the most amount of time in—it's where we get to be visionaries. Or at least pretend we're being visionaries. Either way, it's fun.

In my lexicon, strategizing represents finding all the opportunities to address the trends we've identified under the Analyzer section. We're going to use many of the frames, issue processors and growth principles. And remember, we need to have mindful intent—is this getting me closer while acknowledging my preferences?

The outcome we want is to align all of our actions to get us closer to the things we want. So, before you begin this process, go back through your Solvable Problem™. Open up the CertaintyApp and see how much additional cash you need each year to fund all of your priorities.

As we come up with strategies, can we close the gap to fund all of our priorities entirely? Are the strategies we are developing inherently asymmetric to the upside? If not, how can you eliminate downside risk?

I like to start with the low-hanging fruit by considering the following:

1. Should I cancel all software expenses where the usage is episodic and there are no clear hard cost savings?
2. Should I eliminate all expenses that are marked as non-core and have no cost savings?
3. Can I realign the frequency of each expense with the usage rate? Ideally, we get all expenses to be as flatlined as possible so that monthly profits are more easily determinable.
4. Sort savings from highest to lowest. Do I have a preponderance of data to support my savings projections by expense? For time savings, we often fall into the trap of over-generalized recommendations ("Everything under $200 an hour needs to be outsourced" has a ton of assumptions baked into it).

5. What is my current Profit Time Index (total profits divided by time you spend working in the business)? Is the cost savings on an hourly basis greater than the Profit Time Index? If not, how would I better utilize my time to improve the savings? If I can't, I'll consider canceling the expense.

Now, we examine the data through the lens of the Parenting Frame. The Parenting Frame asks: How can I prevent bad things from happening? Specifically, examine the trends where the outcomes got you further away from where you wanted to be. How did this occur? Were you playing someone else's game? Did you ignore the frames, issue processors or growth principles?

You'll have to dig deep here and apply the Professional Skeptic Frame to each of your answers when you're done. It can be hard to acknowledge where we violated our own rules of the game. It's essential, however, that we are willing to question our assumptions.

Through this series of questions, you will make a list of solutions. Add these to the Four Lenses workbook I describe in the Four Lenses section of the book to evaluate your proposed solutions for asymmetry. You will also evaluate these solutions under the context of never watering the weeds. That is, you'll ask yourself: while this opportunity has asymmetric risk if I implemented it now, would it get me further away from my profit priorities?

Then apply the Commissioner Frame. Remember, the Commissioner Frame asks: If I had to play this game for life, would I be okay with the rules I've set? Based on the rhythm of the business you've created, are you okay with the outcomes? Why or why not?

Are you working with vendors because you thought it

would solve a problem but they are not vendors you'd want to work with in perpetuity?

Did you engineer a business that has a lot of variability in revenue but the expenses skew heavily toward fixed costs?

Do you have a small contribution margin but really high fixed costs so that each month requires you to generate a lot of volume?

Do you consistently add expenses in low revenue months causing you to create losses? What if we implemented stop losses where we capped our spending in those months to be equal to our revenue?

As a side note to this, one of the ways I can double a client's cash flow quickly is by running their profit and loss by month since inception. Then I line up the profits or losses by month (I see profits or losses for every January by year, then every February by year and so on). I sum up all the profits by year and then I change all the loss months to zero. That is, instead of having a loss in those months, the business simply broke even. Interestingly, more times than not, it doubles the business's profitability (often I see a 3-10x increase in profitability). What makes it even more fun is that it is typically during the same three to four months every year.

You've created a business where the rhythm causes you to lose money in the same months every year, and those losses substantially eat away at your profitability. You could instead implement rules to change the game.

Next, I'm going to contemplate where in my business I'm violating this issue processor: First We Optimize, Then We Maximize.

Chances are, as the algorithms work in concert when you violate this issue processor, you made decisions without a preponderance of data, skipped over taking microsteps to validate the idea or tried to scale before you hit your pre-prescribed optimal ratios.

Remember, when you try to maximize, you are defaulting to "more." You're trying to have everything now. In doing so, you allow your inherent biases to take over, thereby allowing yourself to start rationalizing the adding of expenses when the data doesn't support asymmetry, getting further away from your profit priorities or simply losing momentum altogether because your resources are too limited to do everything at once.

As you identify areas where you have been maximizing, consider if the expense can be cut now. If it's not that simple, consider solutions that you'll add to the Four Lenses workbook and filter through the issue processor of never watering the weeds.

Next, evaluate the Rule of Three and 10. The Rule of Three and 10 is especially helpful to gauge future expenses and, more importantly, avoid the cost of having to fix something that's already broken. The hard costs and the cognitive burden costs are especially high when we have to fix something we know we have the tools to avoid.

Now, I haven't forgotten about T-learning over I-learning.

In every solution we develop, we should develop to T-learning where we can likely find solutions that already exist. This is perhaps most effective as you examine the expenses where you have had a long-term relationship with vendors (not transactional). Are there ways you can leverage the relational capital to restructure the deal? When you approach the vendor, remember that this is a relationship. What do we already know about relationships and how to influence outcomes? Draw from that data to inform how to best broach any solutions you develop.

Here are a few examples:

Say you have a marketing provider you've worked with long-term. Can you restructure the agreement so that it's pay-for-performance rather than a fixed monthly fee? In doing so, can you lower the threshold each month to breakeven?

Or, say, for example, you have a long-term relationship with a coach. Could you launch a joint venture project so that they waive their coaching fee?

I've had success with both of these examples. I use it to manufacture the outcomes I need to get closer to my priorities.

I'd be remiss if I didn't remind you that each of these ideas needs to be run through the Four Lenses, as it's unlikely that you'll have the preponderance of data you'll need to bias microsteps in order to validate any solutions you choose. Regardless, when we move away from thinking that *more* is the default answer, then we can find an almost infinite range of solutions to get closer to what we want, and leveraging relational capital tends to be a bastion of asymmetry.

E: Execute

You did all the hard work; now you need to pull the trigger. We need to play our game. Based on your Kolbe A, how is your Follow-Thru? Based on your default tendencies, are you the person to carry everything through to fruition?

You can build an awesome strategy, but if it never gets executed, what is the point? So often, strategizing just dies on the vine.

As Sun Tzu said, "If you know the enemy and know yourself, you need not fear the result of a hundred battles. If you know yourself but not the enemy, for every victory gained you will also suffer a defeat. If you know neither the enemy nor yourself, you will succumb in every battle."

If playing your game is strategizing and providing support, then build that into the execution plan. Find the resources to augment your strengths. Don't build a system that requires you to play someone else's game. That's fragile and likely to fail. Not to mention, you've now built a plan that's inherently asymmetric to the downside: We have to be someone else or this plan fails.

Part of execution is what Stephen Covey in *The 7 Habits of Highly Effective People* called "sharpening the saw." To ensure success while executing and also creating a flywheel for multiplicative growth, you need to unpack all your biases that created these opportunities. What new frames, issue processors and growth principles do you need to add? Or what adjustments to your existing tools need to be made?

Applying the Investor Frame, after you execute all of the above, would you want to buy this business given what it's worth? If not, why? Can these issues that caused you to say no be addressed? If not, stop! Go back to strategy. The strategy now needs to shift to: How can I exit from this business while maximizing my exit without getting further away from my priorities?

Based on all of the above, how much cash are we saving? How will we reinvest this to fund our priorities? Look at your current accounts. What rates of return are those generating?

Say you found $300,000 per year in additional cash, which is a common outcome for a seven-figure business, and that you're only getting .1 percent on it. In 10 years, that balance will be $3,013,536. That's a big number, so this exercise was certainly worth performing. The math nerd in me, however, has to point out that you contributed $3,000,000 of that number ($300,000 per year times 10). You earned a measly $13,536 over 10 years. That's not asymmetry to the upside. Arguably, it's asymmetric to the downside. However, if you consider inflation, you can average around three percent.

By now, you should be calibrated to ask this question: What are other options for this cash that you already have on your Four Lenses list? What are those expected rates of return? How does that change the balance in 10 years?

Does this close the gap on all your priorities? If not, how

much do we need to grow revenues and how can we do it without violating our rules?

Say the outcome from the above is you find solutions with an expected annual average return of 20 percent. That $300,000 per year invested at 20 percent becomes $7,787,605 after 10 years and $56,006,400 after 20 years.

If you're a 40-year-old who spends on average $500,000 (including taxes), the amount you need to retire is somewhere in the range of $12,000,000 to $15,000,000. Now, there's a lot of assumption that goes into that range, so your number could be more or less, but let's assume this as a starting point.

If we didn't do anything more with our business and everything stayed the same except we unlocked this $300,000 in cash and reinvested it in opportunities that generated 20 percent returns, we would reach that $12,000,000 target in 12.1 years and the $15,000,000 target in 13.2 years.

Most of us are so busy targeting "more" that retirement at the age of 65 may not even be possible, and the above shows how even without doing anything extra, you could get there between ages 52.1 and 53.2.

As you bump up the savings or your rate of return, the distance to your target just gets shorter and shorter. It's like legally driving faster on the freeway or taking shortcuts.

18

CONCLUSION

Well, you made it.

You are now armed with the strategies, tools and ways to rig your game.

You no longer have to put in effort for effort's sake. That doesn't mean you won't work hard. Shoot, you'll probably work harder than everyone else you know.

You no longer need to take on *all* the risks to win. Evidence suggests that merely burning the boats is not a guarantee for success. You will take calculated risks and you will now actively work to hedge the downside.

You now have the freedom to leave options open. After all, you don't have to value *more*. And you most certainly don't have to play by anyone else's rules. In fact, if you do try to become someone you're not, you've almost certainly doomed yourself to failure.

You must, however, acknowledge that all of this is part of an infinite game. Goals and uncertainty are ubiquitous parts of business and they make for a daunting combination. As long as you are living and breathing, you will set goals, move the goal-posts and change your thoughts around your wants and needs.

You will find yourself constantly stuck between visions of all the things you want to give yourself and your loved ones and the uncertainty of how you're going to be able to attain those things. What do you do about that?

In those moments, it all comes back to *you*.

You can cultivate clarity through your Solvable Problem™. This is your tool for assessing whether or not you are violating Commandment #1: Closer Over More.

No longer will you lose momentum through fighting a battle of facts when you can stop and honor Commandment #2: Preference versus Binary.

You can now use that newfound clarity to assess Commandment #3: Every Decision Has Infinite Trade-Offs. Given all these trades, you have the freedom to design the life that you want.

Along the way, you will consider Commandment #4: Business Decisions Should Have Asymmetric Upside. As such, you will identify and eliminate risks where you find them, putting aside the idea of raking in more of the things you feel you should be accumulating and focusing on keeping what you already have.

You will do it all by being you. You will play your game. Why? Because only you can play your game. No one else can play your game, so why play someone else's game?

And you will take the 12 core principles herein and you'll metabolize them, thereby making them your own. Through that, you will now create strategies backed by data (a preponderance of data, in fact) that will lead you toward finding the highest-leverage path from where you are to where you want to be.

Now, make no mistake about it: Sometimes you will still fail. And that will be hard. But more often than not, you will proactively prevent bad things from happening. And when you do, you will recover faster.

You will likely discount the value of recovering faster, but the value, for example, of going from being spun out for three months to one month or eight hours to one hour is immense.

Is that all, Dan?

Almost. I want to make a promise to you before you go: If you adopt this methodology as you make your decisions and craft a future for yourself and your business that prioritizes your real ideal outcomes, then you can finally operate from a place of certainty, wealth, purpose and prosperity.

You won't have to do any guesswork. You won't have to worry about your competition. Remember Gary? You can tell Gary to take a hike (edited version).

It's time to start focusing on the tools that will move the needle and get you moving toward a more intentional and actualized version of success.

If you do, dear readers, the game will always be rigged in your favor.

Now get out there and play your game!

"From what we get, we can make a living; what we give, however, makes a life."
—Arthur Ashe

ABOUT THE AUTHOR

A serial entrepreneur since birth, Dan Nicholson took a detour through the "conventional" model of graduating summa cum laude with degrees in accounting and information systems, completing a fellowship at the Governmental Accounting Standards Board, working at Deloitte and various Fortune 500 companies and being named to the 40 Under 40 list of global accountants four times. One day, Dan woke from his cloud of dissonance, tired of the corporate drudgery of meetings about meetings and future meetings. Now, he takes the conventional and applies it to the non-conventional by helping purpose-driven entrepreneurs achieve financial certainty.

Dan is the founder of multiple companies across finance, accounting and software, but his real passion is teaching entrepreneurs and small business owners through his 20-week online course, Certified Certainty Advisor. The course provides practical and effective processes to achieve financial success on your own terms.

Dan lives in Seattle with his wife and two daughters.

Access Additional Free Resources and
Content Using the QR Code Below